FROOME

JOHN MURRAY

DINO

Published by Dino Books
an imprint of John Blake Publishing
3 Bramber Court, 2 Bramber Road,
London W14 9PB, England

www.johnblakebooks.com

www.facebook.com/johnblakebooks 🔲
twitter.com/jblakebooks 🔲

This edition published in 2017

ISBN: 978 1 78 606 466 0

British Library Cataloguing-in-Publication Data:

A catalogue record for this book is available from the British Library.

Design by www.envydesign.co.uk
Cover illustration by Dan Leydon
Background image: Shutterstock

Printed in Great Britain by CPI Group (UK) Ltd

1 3 5 7 9 10 8 6 4 2

Papers used by John Blake Publishing are natural, recyclable products made from
wood grown in sustainable forests. The manufacturing processes conform to the
environmental regulations of the country of origin.

Every attempt has been made to contact the relevant copyright-holders, but some
were unobtainable. We would be grateful if the appropriate people could contact us.

John Blake Publishing is an imprint of Bonnier Publishing.
www.bonnierpublishing.com

For Clare and Beth

TABLE OF CONTENTS

CHAPTER 1

KING OF FRANCE

One hundred and thirteen kilometres to go. That was all that stood between him and victory. The equivalent of riding from London to Southampton. A tough task for any ordinary cyclist, but not for someone who had already ridden more than 3,000 km in the previous three weeks – and that included pedalling up some of the highest mountains in Europe.

Chris smiled and waved to the cheering crowd as he set off from the start line. The sun was out, there was a party atmosphere, and he was going to enjoy each and every one of the 113 km facing him.

The fans screamed their support.

'Go on, Chris.'

'Well done, Froomey.'

'Bring the yellow jersey home for Britain!'

It was the twenty-first and final stage of the 2016 Tour de France, the most famous and most challenging bike race in the whole world, and Chris was on the verge of winning it for the third time. Only seven men in the race's 103-year history had done that before.

While there was still one stage to go, it was tradition that the final leg of the Tour was a procession, where riders would not attack or try to gain time on the race leader. If Chris could stay on his bike, he would win the Tour. His smile grew even bigger when that thought crossed his mind.

As the race leader, Chris wore the yellow jersey – or *maillot jaune*, as the French fans called it – instead of the usual blue of Team Sky. That made it very easy for other riders to spot him.

'You deserve it, mate,' said his former teammate, Australia's Richie Porte, patting him on the back.

'Congratulations, Chris. You were too strong for us this year… but I'll be even stronger next year,' chuckled Romain Bardet, the French cyclist who was second in the overall rankings.

'Thanks, Romain,' Chris laughed. 'I was hoping you might go easy on me!'

It made a pleasant change to have a friendly conversation with his rivals. Chris had spent three weeks locked in a deadly battle with them around the roads of France in his bid to win the Tour. Every day, they had been his enemies.

There had been some unforgettable moments along the mammoth journey, including his daredevil descent down a mountain to win Stage 8 and a thrilling attack during a windy Stage 11 to gain some more precious seconds. There were other moments Chris would have preferred to forget, such as when he crashed on Stage 19 and had to use his teammate Geraint Thomas's bike to get to the finish.

'It was definitely worth all the pain,' Chris said to himself, as he gaped open-mouthed at the thousands upon thousands of fans standing at the side of the road. He could never believe that so many people would come to watch them race. It was one of the things that made the Tour de France extra special.

As he pedalled along, Chris started thinking about how far he had come from the days growing up in Kenya, when he used to ride his old supermarket bike in the hills, looking down on the stunning African landscape, day after day, for hours on end. Back then, who could have imagined that he would become a three-time Tour de France champion?

'Wake up, Froomey. We're coming up to the Champs-Élysées.'

Chris was snapped back to reality by Geraint's voice – or G as the Welsh rider was known by everyone at Team Sky. 'There's still some work to do before we start the celebrations.'

'Sorry, G!'

While much of the final stage was ridden at a gentle pace, the race began in earnest when the riders arrived at the Champs-Élysées. Nine times they would lap around the famous avenue in the centre of Paris, travelling at breakneck speed. Just one mistake here, one crash, and Chris's dream of glory could be ruined.

'Keep your concentration,' Chris said to himself as he cycled past the Arc de Triomphe monument. 'One big last push.'

Chris was surrounded by his Sky teammates. They had played a huge part in his victory, protecting their leader from other riders, chasing down his rivals, and giving him food and drink – or, in G's case, his bike!

The team weren't bothered about winning the individual stage today; all that mattered was making sure Chris reached the finish line safely. He held a four-minute advantage over Romain, so had plenty of time to spare.

As the sprinters tore up the Champs-Élysées one last time, with André Greipel crossing the line first, Team Sky stayed well out of trouble at the back of the main group of cyclists.

With the finish in sight, Chris called out to his teammates.

'Come on, boys. Let's finish this together. This is a victory for our whole team as much as for me. I couldn't have done it without you.'

And with that, the nine cyclists from Team Sky linked arms and rode to the finish in one single line.

Chris had done it. After an exhausting eighty-nine hours in the saddle, he was the Tour de France champion!

He had previously won the Tour in 2013 and 2015 and now he had become the first cyclist in twenty years to retain his title. What an incredible achievement.

'This is the best day of my life,' Chris said after the race, dedicating the victory to his wife Michelle and to his seven-month-old son Kellan, who was there to watch his father win. 'It's an absolutely amazing feeling. To wear the yellow jersey is every cyclist's dream.'

CHAPTER 2

AFRICAN ADVENTURE

'Okay, take it easy, Mr Turkey. I'm your friend.'

The turkey puffed out its feathers in anger. It didn't look like it wanted to be friends. It was the same size as him, probably even bigger.

'Nobody's going to hurt you,' he said slowly, retreating to the back of the cage. 'Will one of you let me out now?' he hissed at his brothers.

Their only response was to laugh.

The turkey looked at him again and gobbled … and then it charged.

'Aaarrrggghhh! Help me!'

Cue more laughter. As the turkey chased their little brother around the dog cage, Jeremy and Jono fell on the floor in hysterics.

'Jeremy... Jono... let me out... please!' Chris screamed while trying to dodge a wing coming straight at his head.

Eventually, Chris's brothers took pity on him and released him from the cage. He stormed off without a word.

Just another typical afternoon in Africa: being attacked by a giant turkey!

Chris and his brothers grew up in a large house called Windy Ridge in a town just outside of Nairobi, the biggest city in Kenya. They lived with their mum Jane and dad Clive, although everyone called him Noz.

They also lived with lots of pets.

In Britain, a typical household might have a couple of cats or maybe a hamster as the family pet, but things were different in Africa. The Froome household was more like a zoo. There were chickens, ducks, geese, dogs, rabbits, horses, cows (which were milked by Jane), a bull, and of course the turkey.

Jeremy also liked collecting snakes, his favourite

being a twelve-foot long python. Unfortunately for Chris, that spelt bad news for his pet rabbits, which sometimes ended up as the python's lunch!

'Has anyone seen my rabbit today?' he asked his family. The guilty look on Jeremy's face confirmed his worst fears.

When he wasn't dodging turkeys or trying to save his rabbits, Chris loved living in Kenya. There was so much to do – particularly for an extremely energetic young boy. He would spend his time climbing trees or making a swing or a slide on the family property. One of his favourite hobbies was catching and collecting butterflies.

If he ever got bored of the family pets, Chris didn't have to go far out of Nairobi to see some other, much bigger – and much more fearsome – animals. Jane often took her youngest son on a drive to one of Kenya's beautiful national parks.

Chris adored these special trips and was so excited each time he spotted an animal.

'Look, there's a lion!'

'Wow, five elephants!'

Sometimes the animals came a little too close for comfort.

'Is that a rhino over there?'

'You mean the huge grey animal with a horn that's heading right towards us?'

'Okay, you'd better keep driving, Mum.'

Jane knew the safari drives well. Her parents were English, but she had grown up in Kenya. Noz, meanwhile, had moved to Kenya from England as a young adult to start a tourism business. He met Jane and loved Africa so much that he decided to build his life there. The family still kept their ties with England, though; Jeremy and Jono – who were a lot older than Chris – went to boarding school there.

It was around this time that life changed for six-year-old Chris. Jane and Noz were arguing a lot. He never wanted to stick around to see his parents fighting, and so – with his brothers away at school – he spent a lot of time on his own.

His only companion was his little black bike.

Hour after hour, day after day, Chris rode his bike around the family property and on the dirt track at the front of the house. He loved practising tricks, pulling wheelies and jumping off ledges – even if this sometimes led to a crash or scraping his knee on the ground. It was all part of the fun!

'I'm going out on my bike, Mum,' he called out.

'Just make sure you're back before it gets dark.'

'Sure thing,' came the reply as he and his bike disappeared into the distance.

Chris always obeyed his mum's rules. He liked to time his return home perfectly – wheeling his bike through the door just as the sun disappeared.

As much as he enjoyed racing around on his bike, sadly things didn't improve at home between Jane and Noz and they decided to separate. Chris was very upset, especially as his father was moving away to South Africa.

Soon Chris was on the move too, leaving behind Windy Ridge and many of the pets for a new home with Jane. He made sure his little black bike was the first thing he packed.

CHAPTER 3

MORE THAN JUST A HOBBY

'If you like cycling that much, you'll have to get a new bike.'

Chris's eyes lit up. A new bike?

'You've been talking about cycling for the last hour, I know you spend every spare moment out on your bike – you're obsessed with it! So, if you want to get serious about cycling, you can't keep riding around on that tiny BMX for the rest of your life.'

Chris knew Noz was right. He could barely get on his bike these days without his feet dragging along the ground.

'What type of bike should I get?' Chris asked. As much as he loved cycling, he didn't know anything about the different types of bikes.

'You need a mountain bike.'

That sounded good to Chris, especially the 'mountain' bit. He enjoyed riding up the Kenyan hills – and loved coming down them again as quickly as possible.

And so Chris and Noz went bike shopping and he returned to Nairobi from his holiday in South Africa with a brand new mountain bike in his luggage.

'Welcome home, Chris,' Jane said with a smile, as she hugged her son at the airport. 'Now, how are we going to fit all this in the car?'

'I'll cycle if you want!'

Chris was even closer to his mum these days. They had formed a special relationship since leaving Windy Ridge. Life was different with just the two of them, and they had lived in several houses around Nairobi, sometimes house-sitting, sometimes staying with his grandparents.

Wherever they went, Chris always took the opportunity to check out the new surroundings on his bike. He loved to feel the heat of the scorching African sun on his face and the wind blowing through his hair, as he sped down hills and skidded around corners. There were always new things to look at and new areas to explore.

Jane was happy that Chris had found a hobby that he so enjoyed but, like any mother, she worried at times.

'Be careful please, Chris, especially going down those hills. I don't want to see you at the hospital.'

As part of her training to be a physio, Jane worked at the local hospital. She had to do very long working hours which, in turn, meant Chris had to spend a lot of hours at school.

Some days, his mum would drop him off at school so early that he would sit on the front steps until the classroom was opened.

'At least this gives me a chance to catch up on some homework,' Chris said to himself as he waited for his classmates to arrive.

Like most schoolchildren, Chris enjoyed some classes more than others. He was good with numbers and did well at maths. In fact, back when they lived at Windy Ridge, he had even used his maths knowledge to sell avocados in the local community after collecting them from the trees in the property. A businessman at six years old!

English lessons were harder, however, as Chris was dyslexic, meaning that he struggled with reading. For a while, he had to take extra classes for reading on a Saturday, which was the last thing he wanted to do when he could have been out on his bike.

On other weekends, though, Chris and his mum would jump in the car and set off on long drives into the African countryside. They would walk in the wilderness, where Chris loved learning about the wildlife and listening to all the different sounds of the African bush. Sometimes they would camp overnight.

Of course, Chris's bike was never too far away. He would put it in the back of the car alongside the camping gear. Once they were out on the open roads, he would take it for a ride, cycling behind his mum's car – and sometimes overtaking it!

Up to this point, his cycling hobby had been exactly that – a hobby, albeit one that he practised a lot. But now he wanted more. He wanted to learn more about cycling, he wanted to ride with other cyclists, he wanted to race.

'I'd like to enter a race, Mum,' Chris said as they drove home from another magical day in the bush.

Jane raised her eyebrows. 'If you want to be a racer, Chris, you're first going to have to learn how to cycle properly. The roads in Kenya are dangerous. You need to learn how to cycle on them safely, how to go around corners properly, how to avoid all the potholes.'

'But who will want to teach me all that?

The answer was David Kinjah.

CHAPTER 4

SAFARI SIMBAZ

Chris felt nervous. Here he was, a thirteen-year-old boy who liked messing around on a BMX and mountain bike, about to meet the captain of the Kenyan national cycling team. He walked towards the man who was wearing the Kenyan cycling kit, the black, green and red colours glistening in the sunlight. He had long dark dreadlocks and cut a tall imposing figure.

'Hi, I'm David Kinjah. Pleased to meet you.'

Chris instantly relaxed as David greeted him with the widest smile he had ever seen.

'Your mother tells me you want to learn about cycling?'

'Yes please.'

Chris had just finished competing in a charity road race and his mum had been there to cheer him on. At the end of the race, Jane had approached David to ask if he could help Chris learn more about cycling. She had heard that the Kenyan captain ran a group teaching local young cyclists. They were called the Safari Simbaz.

Chris liked David straightaway. He took a keen interest in Chris's cycling and asked lots of questions – about his bike, where he cycled and for how long. Chris was only too happy to answer all of them.

'It sounds like you might enjoy cycling with the Safari Simbaz. Why don't you come and ride with us one day?'

'That sounds great. See you soon, David.'

'Please, call me Kinjah.'

'Okay, see you soon, Kinjah!'

Chris thought about the Safari Simbaz all the way home and his excitement increased when he found out more about his new teacher. Kinjah had competed for Kenya at the Commonwealth Games, against some of the best cycling nations on the planet. He had also raced for a professional team in Europe.

But Kinjah's success was a world away from his life in Mai-a-Ihii, a tiny village on the outskirts of Nairobi. His home was a tin hut, made up of one big room that was split in half. On one side of the room was a living room; on the other, a bed, kitchen and lots of bikes.

It was in Mai-a-Ihii where Chris met Kinjah again and was introduced to the Safari Simbaz.

'Hi. My name's Chris,' he introduced himself, smiling. But his fellow cyclists stared blankly at him, and he quickly realised there was a problem – they all spoke Swahili! While Swahili was the main language in East Africa, Chris only knew a handful of words as he had been brought up speaking English.

'It looks like I'm going to have to learn a new language!' he said to himself, keeping his communication to waves and handshakes with the rest of the group.

'So, are you ready to come cycling with us?' asked Kinjah.

Chris had never been more ready. He was unable to speak Swahili, but for now at any rate he would let his cycling do the talking.

The first ride was an experience he would never forget. Up steep hills, down windy roads, across bumpy tracks, along narrow paths, on and on they rode. At the front of the pack was Kinjah, leading the way, his dreadlocks flapping in the wind.

'Where are we going?' Chris asked after a couple of hours.

'Who knows?' Kinjah replied with a grin, and then warned, 'Watch that pothole!'

Chris swerved to avoid the fast-approaching hazard. He had to keep his wits about him – no sooner had they dodged one obstacle than another one was waiting around the corner.

At some point – Chris had no idea when – Kinjah waved his hand and the group stopped.

'Lunch!'

They didn't pull over at the side of the road for a quick bite to eat, as Chris had expected. Instead, they enjoyed lunch with some of Kinjah's relatives who lived in another village. Chris was handed a bowl of something that looked like porridge. He didn't know what it was, but it tasted delicious. He was so hungry after the morning's cycling and ate every last spoonful.

'Right, back on the bikes.'

It was time to go, time for another thrilling adventure. Chris didn't know where they were going, but he didn't care. He was having too much fun.

Eventually, six hours after they had set out from Mai-a-Ihii, the Safari Simbaz were back at Kinjah's hut. Chris was exhausted. What a day. He had never ridden for so long. It had been hard and, at times, the group had slowed down to wait for him, but he had survived. And nothing could remove the smile from his face.

'Well done today,' Kinjah said. 'I was really impressed by your efforts, especially as it was your first time. Will you be joining us again?'

'Just try and stop me!'

From that day onwards, that was how Chris spent

much of his holidays. Day after day after day. Several
of the Safari Simbaz would stay the night in Kinjah's
home, lying side by side on the big bed, and it wasn't
long before Chris started doing the same.

Jane wasn't worried if her son didn't come home
every evening. She knew he was well looked after by
Kinjah and was doing what he loved. And the more
time Chris spent there, the more he was accepted by
the group. His Swahili quickly improved and he was
soon cracking jokes with his new friends at the end
of a long day's cycling.

They even had a name for him – *Murungaru.*

'What does that mean?' Chris asked Kinjah.

Kinjah laughed. 'They call you the "gangly kid".'

Chris didn't mind one bit. Having a proper
nickname made him feel like he was part of the
group. Besides, his teammates were right. He *was* a
bit gangly. Kinjah explained that if he wanted to be a
top cyclist, he would have to develop more muscle.

Chris also learned about the bikes. Kinjah was
an expert at repairing bikes and would often give
the other cyclists tips to help them ride faster. It

might be fixing a wheel, moving the handlebars or adjusting the height of the saddle – it was all useful information and Chris absorbed every word of it.

There was one other word he absorbed too.

'Come on, Chris, keep going. *Harambee*,' Kinjah said one day during a particularly tricky climb.

'*Harambee*. What does that mean?' gasped Chris between breaths.

'It's a Swahili word meaning "Let's all pull together". And that's what the Safari Simbaz do for each other. We're a team.'

Chris managed a quick smile through the pain. It felt amazing to be part of a team.

CHAPTER 5

GOING SOUTH

'We've decided that you're going to leave your school…'

Sorry?

'To go to boarding school…'

Hang on a minute.

'In South Africa.'

Whhhaaattt?

Chris's new adventures with Kinjah and the Safari Simbaz were only just underway, and now his life was turned upside down again. On one of his visits to see Noz in Johannesburg, his dad broke the news to him. Secondary school in Kenya was very expensive, and so his parents had decided he should continue his education in South Africa.

And that was that. Decision made.

This came as a massive shock to Chris. He thought of all the things he would have to leave behind – his mum, his mates, the beautiful Kenyan countryside and, of course, Kinjah.

'Don't worry, son,' Noz said. 'Kenya's not going anywhere. Everything will be here when you come back.'

'But what about cycling with the Safari Simbaz?'

'They won't forget you – you'll be able to ride with them in the holidays. Besides, I bet there's a cycling club at your new school.'

For the first time that day, there was a smile on Chris's face.

Unfortunately, that smile would soon disappear – when he arrived at his new school, St Andrew's, at the age of fourteen, he discovered that not only was cycling frowned upon, but the weather was absolutely freezing.

'Welcome to Bloemfontein,' a pupil shouted out as Chris shivered his way through the front gates.

'Bloem-what?'

'Bloemfontein,' the boy laughed. 'It's the nearest city to our school. It's pronounced Bloom-font-eyn.'

'More like *blooming* freezing.'

Chris had never felt so cold in his life. He was used to the warmth of Nairobi, not South Africa in the middle of winter, and he didn't have any suitable clothes to wear.

It was not a good start, and it didn't get any better. Everything at St Andrew's School was built around rules. Chris had to go to chapel every day. He had to make sure his bed and the dorm room he shared with another pupil were spotless. He was not allowed to make a sound at night once the lights had gone out.

Rules, rules and more rules.

If the school was strict with its rules, it was even stricter when pupils disobeyed them. Punishments were carried out by the older boys, who were called prefects. More often than not, they involved physical exercise.

'Froome, get down on your hands and knees and give me twenty press-ups.'

'Ten laps of the rugby field, Froome.'

'What took you so long? Five more laps.'

Fortunately, Chris was very fit from all his cycling, so he could just about cope with the exercise demands, but that didn't mean he enjoyed it. Even so, he was determined to get on with it as best he could.

'Don't give in,' he told himself as he did another star jump. 'It's just like those days on the bike with Kinjah – keep going to the end. You're not a quitter.'

It wasn't any easier in the classroom either. At St Andrew's, everyone spoke Afrikaans.

'Not another new language,' Chris thought as he struggled to understand his teachers. 'I've only just started to get to grips with Swahili.'

While Chris was having problems settling into his new life, things were also proving tricky for Jane back in Kenya – thanks to the two special friends her son had left behind. Rocky and Shandy were Chris's two pet pythons; when he moved to South Africa, there was no chance the school would let him bring the snakes, so it was left to Jane to look after them.

Jane had never been a big fan of Rocky and Shandy, and had been happy to let Chris take care of them, especially when it came to their diets. The pythons' main food of choice was live animals, which meant Chris would often have to go out to catch mice, rats or whatever other creatures he could find.

When they weren't eating or sleeping, the snakes would sometimes escape from their cage and roam around the house until Chris found them again – or until they found Jane! Chris would never forget the day when his mum woke up to discover Rocky in her bed.

As time went by, Rocky and Shandy grew so long that they became too big for their cage, and it was decided that they should be released into the wild. Jane certainly wasn't complaining.

Having a pet might have been out of the question at St Andrew's, but Chris was not prepared to let the school's strict ways interfere with his cycling dream. He bought a stunt bike. He wouldn't have lasted two minutes on it cycling up a hill with Kinjah and the Safari Simbaz but, for the purposes of messing around at school, it was perfect … on the rare occasions that he was actually allowed to mess around, of course.

His highlight of the week came on a Saturday afternoon when he could jump on his bike, escape from the school gates and ride over to the houses of his friends who weren't boarders.

Free at last.

He would disappear for hours. The only rule was that he had to be back at school in time for a roll call with one of the dastardly prefects.

Chris pushed himself as hard as he could. He put every last bit of energy into his pedals and would even take a longer or steeper route just to challenge himself.

Those rides were rare moments of fun, and it wasn't long before Noz decided that his son should leave St Andrew's.

'Right, this school's not right for you. We're going to move you again.'

But this time, Chris didn't utter a single word of protest.

CHAPTER 6

MORNING, NOON AND NIGHT

Crunch!

Chris was knocked flat on his back. His whole body ached as he fought to get his breath back.

'Where am I?' he mumbled.

No one answered. He closed his eyes. By the time he came to his senses and looked around, the ball and all the players were at the other end of the pitch.

'Ouch,' he said, rubbing his shoulder. 'I don't think rugby's for me.'

Rugby might have not been the sport of choice for Chris but, at his new school, it was a way of life.

Noz had decided that Chris should move to a school much nearer to him in Johannesburg. After passing his entrance exam with flying colours, Chris was enrolled at St John's College.

To his enormous relief, everything was a lot more relaxed at his new boarding school – and he didn't have to do fifty press-ups every time he forgot to make his bed!

Playing rugby provided its own kind of punishment, however. It wasn't that Chris didn't like the sport – he threw himself into each match with typical enthusiasm – but his tall, thin frame was no match for his muscular, heavier schoolmates. Particularly when they charged right at him.

It wasn't long before Chris worked out that, to survive school with all his limbs intact, it might be best to steer clear of the rugby field. His heart, of course, lay in a different sport and this was another reason why St John's was so appealing – it had its very own cycling club.

'Do you fancy joining us for a ride today, Chris?' asked Matt Beckett one Friday afternoon. Matt was the leader of the club.

'Can't wait.'

'Well, let's hope we're not waiting for you riding *that* thing,' Matt grinned as he pointed at Chris's bike.

'Don't worry, I'll be fine.'

Chris *was* worried, though. While all his new teammates had flash road bikes, he was stuck on his old mountain bike. How would he keep up?

He tried to appear calm.

The team set off at a blistering pace. As they swept around the roads of Jo'burg – as they called it – Chris soon found himself at the back of the group. He was pedalling ferociously, but couldn't gain any ground.

'It doesn't even look like they're trying and they're going faster than me,' he thought.

He refused to be left behind, though. He dug in. Whenever a slight gap opened up, he pedalled even harder to close it. Time and again, the group would pull away, but each time Chris dragged himself back.

Finally, after two hours, the team returned to St John's – all in one group, just how they had started.

'Great ride, Chris,' Matt said afterwards. 'I thought we were going to lose you at one point, but you showed real guts.'

Chris beamed. He had won Matt's respect.

Over the weeks and months that followed, Matt discovered just how gutsy Chris was. They were always out on their bikes together. Riding once a week on a Friday wasn't anything like enough for the two fanatics, so they began cycling almost every afternoon, with the only school rule being they had to be back before dark.

They quickly formed a strong friendship. As a relative newcomer to the sport, Chris had lots to learn and Matt had plenty of helpful tips.

'How do you get such strong legs?' he asked.

'That comes from training, mate. Lots and lots of training.'

'In that case, we need to cycle more then!'

Chris was becoming really serious about cycling. He was obsessed. While he did well at school, studying wasn't his main passion – he wanted to become a professional cyclist.

When he wasn't doing schoolwork, Chris dedicated any spare waking hours to his bike. He created his own mini training gym in his bedroom, setting up his bike on rollers, which meant he could ride indoors for hours on end. While his friends were watching TV in the common room, Chris would be churning out hundreds of kilometres without leaving his room, the only sound being the constant whirring of the wheels.

It helped that Mr Laing – who was in charge of Chris's boarding house – was a big cycling fan and was happy to let his pupil follow his dream, as long as he got his homework done on time.

While the new regime improved Chris's fitness, nothing could beat the real thing of cycling on the road. But there simply weren't enough hours in the day, and so he came up with a plan, which he shared with Matt.

'I've got it! We'll ride in the night.'

'Erm, Chris, are you feeling okay?'

'It's perfect, Matt. We'll get up early each morning, go for a ride, and make sure I'm back in time for breakfast. No one will be any the wiser.'

At 4.30 a.m., Chris's alarm would go off, he'd pull on some clothes and sneak out of his boarding house to fetch his bike. It was often pitch black and absolutely freezing, but nothing could stop him from jumping out of bed each morning.

He would meet Matt, who was a day pupil and lived at home, and the two friends would pedal through the empty streets of Jo'burg as the sun slowly rose.

Sometimes, they stayed out too long and Chris would have to rush back late for breakfast, his face pouring with sweat.

'Why are you so wet, Froome?' asked Mr Laing, as Chris burst through the door of the dining room.

'Sorry sir, I've just got out of the shower!'

Mr Laing smiled and said no more.

CHAPTER 7

UP AND AWAY

'Guess who's back?'

Chris burst through the door of Kinjah's hut.

'Ah, the South African schoolboy returns!' Kinjah's giant smile lit up the room. He was delighted to see his pupil again.

Five months had passed since Chris last set foot in Mai-a-Ihii, but he wasted no time in reacquainting himself with the Safari Simbaz. The day after dropping off his bags at home and catching up with his mum, he headed off to see his friends. Jane didn't mind. It was pointless trying to stand in the way of her son and his bike.

While greeting the other members of the Safari Simbaz, Chris looked around Kinjah's hut. 'This is

44

a bit different to St John's,' he thought. There was no running water or electricity, and it lacked all the modern appliances Chris was used to at his school – but as soon as he walked into the hut, he was at ease. It felt like he was home.

Chris knew he was very lucky to attend such a good school. His teammates in the Safari Simbaz came from very different backgrounds and didn't have that opportunity. But that didn't mean they couldn't be friends; after all, they shared one overriding passion – a love of cycling.

Chris couldn't wait to get back on the road with them.

'Where are we going today, Kinjah? What are we going to see?'

'Plenty, my friend, but first of all we'll see what you've learned on your bike over the last few months.'

Off they rode, up and away into the forests of the Rift Valley. Chris sucked in the clean mountain air, and the flat streets of Jo'burg – and all the traffic fumes – felt a million miles away. Back in the city, Chris would have raced Matt as they weaved between the cars. But up in the Ngong Hills, he had more chance of bumping into a baboon or a giraffe than a vehicle!

In his early days with the Safari Simbaz, Chris was stuck at the back of the group, worrying that he was about to be abandoned and left at the mercy of Kenya's fiercest animals. But Kinjah was always on hand with another valuable lesson.

'Make sure you position your bike behind another rider. That way, their body will act as a windshield for you, meaning you use 20 per cent less energy. That makes it easier for you to keep up with them.'

'That's a great tip, thank you.'

'Don't thank me – thank your teammates. They'll be doing the hard work for you. When you develop, it will be your turn to ride at the front while they have a rest behind you.'

Chris was a quick learner and hungry to take in as much information as possible. As time went by and he put in more and more hours of training in his bedroom, he grew fitter too. He was no longer stuck at the back. Each time he returned from St John's, he would be a little bit stronger than his teammates.

Well, all but one of them.

Kinjah remained a class apart.

Chris drew inspiration from watching Kinjah. He dreamed of being at the front of the group, leading the team up the hills.

One day, he decided to test himself against the Safari Simbaz leader.

'Last one back home makes dinner,' he shouted as he sped off into the distance.

At least he thought he was in the distance.

When he turned around a minute later to check how far back Kinjah was, he was astonished to see his mentor right on his shoulder. Worse still, he was barely breaking sweat.

'Not today, my friend,' Kinjah laughed. 'I'm feeling hungry so let's hope you cook something nice!'

And with that, he was gone. Before long, all Chris could see were those familiar dreadlocks on the horizon.

'Maybe next time,' he muttered.

While he couldn't match Kinjah's speed or strength, Chris did hold one small advantage – he had no fear. He didn't know the meaning of the word. There were some hills in the Rift Valley that were too dangerous even for Kinjah, but Chris carried on undaunted.

'Race you down the hill?'

'No thanks. I'll be taking this one very slowly. I'd like to get home in one piece.'

'Fine. See you at the bottom in ten minutes.'

Ten minutes later, as Kinjah safely wheeled his bike down the treacherous slopes, Chris was nowhere to be seen. Out of the corner of his eye, he spotted a bike at the side of the road. Then a head appeared.

'Give me a hand here please!' yelled Chris.

Kinjah dashed over to find his pupil looking very wet and sorry for himself. He had taken the final corner of the hill too fast, had come off his bike, and fallen in a stream.

'You've still got a lot to learn, my friend,' he said as he dragged him onto dry land. 'Sometimes it helps to be a little afraid.'

Increasingly, it would just be the two of them
out on the road. The stronger Chris became, the
further they would cycle – eight, nine, even ten
hours of pedalling. He would often be on the point
of exhaustion, but he never stopped and refused to
complain.

'What's there to complain about?' he thought. 'I'm
out here doing something I love.'

Kinjah was very impressed with Chris's attitude
and recognised that he had a special talent. Now it
was time to turn that talent into something special.

'Chris, you are one of the toughest riders I
have seen. You never give up and are able to keep
climbing hills when others would stop and walk. But
that alone is not enough to make you a top cyclist –
you need to learn how to race.'

CHAPTER 8

BOY RACER

The rider in the white jersey surged up the mountain. He stood up from his saddle, gritted his teeth and pedalled with all his might. Behind him, the other cyclists winced, unable to keep up with the fierce pace.

Suddenly, a rider in yellow burst out from the pack, powering up the road until he locked onto the back wheel of the white jersey's bike. From then on, the two cyclists fought their own separate battle. One would attack, the other would respond. The man in yellow would open up a five-metre gap, only for his rival in white to sprint past him. On and on it went up the mountain, a series of cat-and-mouse attacks on the steepest hill Chris had ever seen.

He was hooked and couldn't take his eyes off the TV screen.

'What *is* this race?' he asked Matt who was sitting beside him. The friends were spending a rare afternoon off their bikes, although Chris was planning to make up for it by doing three hours on the rollers in his room later.

'The Tour de France. It's the greatest cycling race in the world. The competitors ride around the whole of France. It's so famous that everyone knows it just as "The Tour".'

'It's incredible,' Chris mumbled, his mouth agape as he watched the two cyclists sprint along the narrow mountain road, carving a route through hundreds – no, thousands – of spectators.

The fans were going mad. They wore face paints and colourful clothing, and ran along the road beside the riders, shouting and waving flags. Chris even spotted one person dressed as a red devil. They were so close to the riders they could reach out and touch them.

As always when it came to cycling, Chris had

plenty of questions. As a keen follower of the sport, Matt could provide the answers.

'Why's that guy wearing a yellow jersey?'

'He's the overall leader of the race.'

'Who's the rider in the white jersey?'

'That's Ivan Basso. He's wearing white because he has the leading time out of all the young riders in the Tour.'

'How long does the Tour last?'

'Three weeks.'

'Three weeks of constant cycling? No way.'

'Yes, three weeks. Any more questions or can we watch the race now?'

Chris kept staring at the screen. He was transfixed by Ivan Basso, who was flying up one of the world's steepest mountains as easily as if he was out for a gentle ride around the flat roads of Jo'burg. What a rider.

'Basso is twenty-four, only seven years older than us,' Matt added.

'I'm going to ride in the Tour by the time I'm twenty-four,' Chris said, barely realising he was talking out loud.

Matt laughed. 'Steady on, mate. You haven't even entered a proper race yet!'

That was about to change, however. After Kinjah had urged him to take the next step in his cycling development, Chris had done some research into where he could compete in races. The answer lay not in Nairobi, but back at St John's.

'You should join the Super C Club Academy, which is run by the father of one of your fellow pupils,' said Mr Laing. 'They take part in races practically every weekend.'

Chris and Matt signed up the very next day. It felt great to be a member of a proper, organised team. Chris had been part of the St John's cycling club, and of course there was Kinjah's Safari Simbaz, but this was his first official group membership.

Racing was a very different experience from going out for a training ride. First of all, there was the challenge of getting to the start line – which was sometimes one or two hours' drive away. Not quite as easy as just pedalling out of the school gate for a ride.

Noz took on the role of Chris's chauffeur every

Saturday, sometimes waking up before dawn to get his son to a race in time. He never complained about the early starts or the long drives – apart from the time Chris realised he had left his racing shoes at home one hour into the journey!

'Sorry, Dad,' Chris mumbled as Noz spun the car round.

'I reckon if we get a move on we can make it home and back in time for the start of the race,' Noz replied as he sped down the highway. 'Or if not, you'll have to catch everyone up on your bike!'

'Easier said than done,' thought Chris. He was up against the best teenage riders in the country. Some of them looked like fully-grown men.

'If he's a junior, then I must still be in nappies,' Chris said to Matt one day before the start of the Junior Tour of South Africa, pointing at the cyclist next along in the line, who towered over them both.

'He's got a beard,' he hissed. 'How are we expected to beat him?'

For once, Matt didn't have an answer.

The races were a steep learning curve for Chris.

While he was comfortable in a one-on-one race with Matt or cycling in his room, facing 1,000 or 2,000 other riders was a much more daunting challenge.

'I've got so much to learn, Noz,' he said one day on the drive back home, after finishing in the middle of the field.

A succession of thoughts tumbled out of his mouth. 'Where should I position my bike? When should I make a break? When should I sit in the pack?'

Noz smiled at his son's enthusiasm. 'All in good time, son. Whenever you enter a race, you'll gain more experience and one day soon I'm sure you'll know all the answers.'

Chris was heartened by his dad's reply but he wanted the answers right away. It wasn't that he was doing badly – he always finished and often recorded some decent placings – but he wanted to be the best.

One thing he did know was that the longer and harder the race, the better he performed. While other riders suffered, he actually enjoyed the pain.

But Chris decided to keep that thought to himself. He didn't want to scare Noz!

CHAPTER 9

CHANGING TIMES

Chris took a deep breath before he spoke: 'It costs 10,000 rand.'

'Excuse me! How much?' said Noz, his voice getting louder with every word.

That wasn't quite the response Chris had hoped for. He tried again.

'Erm, 10,000 rand. It's a Colnago – one of the best road bikes you can get. It's a bargain really, you see…' His words trailed off.

'Well, bargain or no bargain, 10,000 rand is a lot of money. You'd better start saving!'

Chris gave his dad a now familiar steely look. 'I'll start today.'

It was no secret that Chris needed a new bike.

While all his rivals in the junior races owned road bikes, Chris was still competing on his old supermarket mountain bike. It put him at an instant disadvantage. If he wanted to give himself a fair chance, the mountain bike would have to be replaced.

Keen to raise the funds as quickly as possible, he started working in a bike shop in Jo'burg on weekends. After each trip to Kenya, he would also bring gifts and clothing back to St John's – and sell them to his schoolmates for a profit. As Noz had pointed out, though, 10,000 rand was a lot of money – the equivalent of 1,000 English pounds at the time – and saving took a long time. Finally, after eight months, Chris had saved enough to buy his beloved Colnago.

'It's beautiful,' he said to Matt as they stared at the blue-and-pink bike in front of them. 'I could look at it all day.'

'Well, you're not going to win any races by looking at it,' Matt chuckled. 'Let's get out there and see how fast you really are!'

As excited as Chris was with his new purchase, Kinjah had warned him that even the best bike would only take him so far. 'You can have the fastest bike in the whole world, but ultimately if you want to be the best rider, it's nothing to do with the bike or equipment; it's down to you.'

They might have been 4,000 km apart, but Kinjah was still regularly in touch with his star pupil. He often sent Chris emails with tips about what to eat (and what not to eat) or how to sit properly on his bike. And if Chris didn't hear anything for a few days, since Kinjah didn't always have access to a computer, he would take matters into his own hands and ask his mum to drive up and see Kinjah herself.

Around the same time, Chris decided to move on from the Super C Club Academy. He'd enjoyed the junior races every Saturday and the fun atmosphere, but if he was serious about his cycling ambitions – and really wanted to take part in the Tour de France one day – he needed a tougher challenge.

Robbie Nilsen was the man to provide that challenge. Robbie ran the Hi-Q Supercycling

Academy, a new club that he had set up in Jo'burg. The pair hit if off instantly.

'We're serious about racing,' Robbie told Chris. 'We enter our academy riders in races all around South Africa – not just short events on flat roads, but up hills and mountains in races as long as 200 km.'

Hills and mountains? Those words were music to Chris's ears. The academy was clearly the real deal.

'So, do you fancy joining us?'

Chris didn't need to be asked twice.

Robbie also had some valuable advice for his academy's newest recruit.

'Training is just as important as racing, probably even more so. And the best way for you to train will be alone,' he said.

Chris looked puzzled. 'I thought you were always meant to train in a group?'

'That is exactly the problem! If you always train with others, you only go as fast as the weakest cyclist allows. The one person who can bring the best out of yourself is you. From now on, it's you, your bike and the big open road.'

From that day on, Chris changed his regime. He was on his own. Crucially, that meant he was now in control of his training – he and he alone would decide the routes, the distances and the numbers of hours in the saddle each day. With Robbie's words burning in his ears, he pushed himself to the maximum.

At times, his legs screamed at him to stop: 'Come on, Chris, you've had a good ride today. Let's skip this last hill and go home.'

But his mind refused to give in: 'Don't let the pain win. What's one more hill?'

'No, the same hill will be here tomorrow. Why don't you give the legs a well-deserved rest?'

His mind always won. 'One more hill.'

Sadly, the new solo regime meant Chris saw a lot less of Matt, especially as their school days at St John's were over. Matt understood – as good friends do.

'Make sure you stay in touch, Chris, and spare a thought for me when you're winning the Tour de France one day!'

Chris laughed. 'I wish!'

With proper equipment, a new training plan and the expert advice of Robbie and Kinjah, Chris was now in a position to give his all to cycling. However, there was just one small obstacle standing in the way – university.

Chris had won a place at the University of Johannesburg but he felt that he wouldn't be able to commit to his studies if he was out on his bike up to eight hours a day. Understandably, his parents were keen for him to pursue his education – there were no guarantees of making a living in cycling.

Something had to give. Eventually, Chris agreed a compromise with his mum and dad where he would delay going to university to focus on his cycling with the academy.

He rang Robbie to tell him the good news. 'Let's go racing!'

Chris spent much of 2005 racing around South Africa. When he went back to Kenya, it was the same story – more races. Most of the events were on flat roads, not the long, hilly courses that suited

Chris's style, but it was invaluable experience, even if he wasn't winning.

The Tour de France remained a very distant dream, but he did get his first taste of a proper tour when the Hi-Q Supercycling Academy entered a team in the Tour of Mauritius.

It was a huge adventure for Chris: his first time overseas with the team. Six days of racing on a beautiful island. As always before any race, Chris studied the map of the course to the finest detail. Each day, they would ride one stage. He was particularly excited about the second stage, which would take the riders on a steep climb up towards a volcano.

'Six hundred metres of climbing – perfect. This could be my chance,' he thought as everyone set off from the start line. He knew it would be a tough day – but for Chris, the tougher, the better.

As the main group of riders slowly edged their way up the mountain, Chris felt strong. He looked around at the other competitors and saw the pained expressions on their faces.

'Now or never, Chris,' he told himself.

He put his head down and pedalled as hard as he could.

'Keep pushing.'

After one minute of intense effort, he finally dared to turn around. There was no one near him!

'Keep pushing. It's not over yet.'

His legs ached. That familiar painful feeling returned. The easy option was to slow down and return to the main group. But 'easy' wasn't a word in Chris's vocabulary.

'Don't let the pain win.'

With every pedal, Chris edged a little closer to victory. Finally, the banner of the finish line came into sight. He took one last look around. No one could catch him now. This made all the solo training rides worthwhile. He took his hands off the bars and raised them above his head.

Chris had won his first stage race!

CHAPTER 10

NATIONAL DUTY

Dear Mr Froome,

It is our great pleasure to confirm that you have been selected to represent Kenya in the 2006 Commonwealth Games in Melbourne.

'No way!' Chris shouted as he dropped the letter in disbelief. He thumped the air in delight. Then, suddenly doubting himself, he picked up the letter again.

He read those seven magical words once more: *You have been selected to represent Kenya.*

There was no mistaking it.

Every sportsperson dreams of competing for their country. Now Chris would have his wish granted – not at any old competition, but the Commonwealth

Games, one of the world's biggest sporting events. He beamed with pride.

After enjoying some encouraging results with the Hi-Q Supercycling Academy team, he had caught the eye of the national selectors and been chosen for the road race and time trial events, along with Kinjah and four other Kenyan riders.

By the time Chris arrived in Australia for the Games, his excitement had increased tenfold. Kinjah had spent the whole journey to Melbourne telling stories of when he had competed at the Commonwealth Games in Manchester four years earlier. The thrill of competing against the world's best athletes, the pride of racing for your country, the wild support of the fans – to Chris, it all sounded too good to be true.

But that bubble was burst within minutes of their arrival in Melbourne.

'Erm, Chris, how are your mountain biking skills?' asked Kinjah, who was staring at the competition entry lists in their room.

'What do you mean?' Chris asked slowly. 'I haven't been on my mountain bike for years.'

'Well, I hope you can remember how to ride it! It says here that, as well as being entered into the road race and time trial, you and I are in the mountain bike competition as well.'

Chris stared at Kinjah in horror. 'Oh no. This must be a mistake.'

After a couple of phone calls and a heated conversation, they found out that there was no mistake at all. The Kenyan Cycling Federation *had* officially entered Chris and Kinjah into the mountain bike event, not realising that cycling on an off-road mud track was very different from cycling along a road. A mud track with bumps, jumps and potholes required different skills.

Seeing Chris's concern, Kinjah tried to reassure his pupil. 'Forget about it. Let's worry about the mountain biking later. Right now, we need to start thinking about tomorrow's time trial.'

Then it was time for Kinjah's next bombshell. 'Oh, by the way, you'll be the first rider to go in the race,' he said casually.

'Whhhaaattt?'

Chris couldn't believe it. Millions upon millions of people would be watching the time trial on TV, and they would all be taking a keen interest in the first rider on the course – a certain Chris Froome from Kenya. He could already feel his legs jangling with nerves.

It was tradition for the slowest rider to go first in the time trial – the organisers had predicted that Chris was the weakest out of all seventy-three entrants.

Chris was furious, and he was still fuming as he prepared to start his time trial the next day.

'Slowest rider. What do they know? I'll show them,' he muttered. He was so angry that any nerves had long since disappeared.

Beep beep beeeeeepppppp.

He was off.

The time trial is very different from the road race in that each rider races against the clock. Setting off two minutes after each other, riders go as fast as they can over the course, and the one with the quickest time wins.

Over the next hour, Chris did everything in his power to prove the organisers wrong. He pedalled like his life depended on it, flying around corners, braking at the last possible second down hills.

It was a great ride. The clock stopped at fifty-three minutes and fifty-eight seconds. Now he had to wait to see who would overtake him.

The next rider failed to beat Chris's time.

'Phew, that's a relief,' he thought. 'At least I won't finish last!'

The third rider was also slower ... and the next ... and the next ...

Every couple of minutes, another competitor would cross the finish line, but still no one could better Chris's time. Not even Kinjah.

In all, forty-nine riders came and went before Chris was eventually knocked off top spot. In the end, he finished seventeenth out of seventy-three riders – an incredible effort and a terrific result for Kenya.

The first person who called Chris after the race was his mum who, as a born-and-bred Kenyan, was absolutely thrilled.

'Everyone is talking about your result back home, Chris. You've done our country proud.'

'Thanks, Mum.'

'I can't wait to watch you competing again.'

'Maybe best if you give the mountain biking a miss!'

But the mountain bike mix-up couldn't put a dampener on Chris's Commonwealth Games experience. Chris and Kinjah both got around the course just about in one piece – once the Kenyan team had found proper bikes for them to ride. Where they finished didn't matter – they had survived.

A few days later, a little bit sore from all the bumps and bruises, they were back in the saddle as part of the road race team. It was another strong performance from Chris, who finished in twenty-fifth place, two places ahead of Kinjah.

Chris might not have won a medal, but he was blown away by the atmosphere and the support of the fans who yelled and cheered non-stop for four hours.

'Go on, Kenya.'

'Keep going, Chris.'

'Hey, that's the young guy who surprised everyone in the time trial. Watch out for him one day.'

At the finish line, Chris noticed a man who was deep in conversation with a colleague. Every so often, he would look up and point directly at Chris.

'Do you know who that man over there is, Kinjah?'

'That, my friend, is none other than Dave Brailsford. He is the head of the British cycling team.'

'Oh right,' Chris replied, thinking he must have been pointing at someone else.

'I understand he is going to start a road cycling team one day. He's looking for potential riders and the word is he has been extremely impressed by your performances.'

CHAPTER 11

EUROPE BECKONS

'If you want to make it in professional racing, you have to get out of Kenya,' said Kinjah as he wheeled his bike into the hut.

Chris was stunned into silence. They had just returned from a typically energy-sapping ride in the Ngong hills, and here was Kinjah – the captain of the national team, the face of Kenyan cycling – telling him to leave his country behind.

'I love cycling here,' he continued, 'but you know as well as I do that the roads are not good to ride on. They're unsafe. Every time you go around a corner, you come across a new hazard – or if you're really unlucky, a lion!'

Chris laughed, but deep down he knew it was

no laughing matter. He needed to race and train in the best conditions and have an elite support team around him. And that was something that Kenya couldn't offer him – as he had found out to his cost at the 2006 Under-23 World Championships in Salzburg, Austria.

Chris had been keen to test himself against the world's best riders in his age group and had sent in an entry form. Unlike the Commonwealth Games, however, he was on his own in Salzburg. Completely on his own. No Kinjah, no other riders, no support team, no one. That meant there was no one to fix his bike if there was a problem or if he got a puncture during the race; there was no one to give him advice over the team radio; there was no one to hand him food or a fresh bottle of water.

It was important for Chris to get off to the best possible start in Salzburg. In the time trial, eager to follow up on his impressive showing in Melbourne, he was pumped up as he waited for the familiar starting beeps.

He exploded out of the start gate, down the ramp, along the first stretch of road and…

CRASH!

Chris rode straight into a race marshal who was wandering across his path. They both tumbled to the floor. Although Chris managed to pick himself up and continue, his race was ruined. He was so embarrassed. It was his first ever race in Europe and, within ten seconds, he was on the tarmac.

Other riders might have been tempted to jump on the next plane home after such a mishap, but that wasn't in Chris's nature. Once he had found out that the marshal was okay, he was determined to regain some pride in the road race. He bounced back remarkably well to finish in the leading group. His performance was all the more impressive given he didn't have anyone to help him.

At the end of the week, he returned home with several valuable lessons – as well as a new nickname from some of his fellow competitors. Chris Froome was now known as Crash Froome.

The whole experience in Austria confirmed to

Chris what Kinjah had been saying. It was time to move on from Kenya, and it was with a heavy heart that Chris said goodbye.

'I can never thank you enough for everything you have done for me, Kinjah,' he said, shaking his mentor's hand. 'Before I met you, I could barely ride a bike. Now I've got my sights set on the Tour de France. I promise to come for a ride whenever I'm back in Kenya.'

'You'd better! Best of luck, Chris. Remember, wherever you go, you'll always be one of the Safari Simbaz.'

Decision made, Chris's next task was to find a team, but first of all he had to head back to university to continue his studies in Jo'burg. He wrote to countless teams, putting forward his case and his strong performances in Melbourne, Salzburg and the Tour of Mauritius. He firmly believed he was good enough to make it in Europe, where all the best teams were based. All he needed was someone to give him an opportunity.

It was a long waiting game. Time dragged by so

slowly, but no one got in touch. The days ticked by at university, and Chris started to fear that he would spend the rest of his days sitting in an office behind a computer screen all day.

Then, suddenly, his luck changed. After weeks without a single phone call, two came along at once – just like London buses!

First, the UCI – the organisation that runs world cycling – invited him to race for their mixed continental team in 2007.

No sooner had Chris accepted that offer than his phone rang again.

'Hi Chris, it's John Robertson from Team Konica Minolta.'

Konica Minolta was a team popular with African riders. John was the team boss and had been impressed by Chris's road race performance in Salzburg. It just so happened that there was one spare spot on his team's roster.

'We'd like to take a chance on you, Chris. Do you fancy joining our team?'

'I'd love to, John, but there's one small problem.

I've signed up to the UCI team for next year already.'

'No problem at all. You can race for both of us.'

It was decided. Chris was now a member of not one, but two teams. It was agreed that he would split his time in 2007 between the teams.

Chris was over the moon. He was going to race alongside the world's best cyclists in Europe. There would be no going back to his economics degree at the University of Johannesburg. And this time, his parents didn't mind one bit.

CHAPTER 12

THAT WINNING FEELING

'If you think the mountains in Kenya are big, wait until you hit the French Alps,' John Robertson said to Chris before training one morning at their base in Belgium.

Chris tried not to look alarmed. His first month with Team Konica Minolta had been a very steep learning curve – and by the sound of things, the mountains were going to be very steep too.

Chris had learned so much from Kinjah and Robbie back in Africa, but being a cyclist in Europe was like starting a completely new subject at school.

When developing their riders, Konica Minolta understood that the best cyclists wouldn't stick around forever but would be snapped up by the really big teams. In the time they did have together, they wanted to bring the best out of them.

John was keen to get his new recruit up to speed as quickly as possible.

First of all, there was the matter of Chris's bike…

'Your bike is too small for you. You're not a teenager any more. You need a new one.'

Then there was what he did when he was on the bike…

'We need to work on your technical skills, like your bike handling and positioning.'

And when he was going downhill…

'Lots of riders are nervous and don't take enough risks when descending – you take too many!'

Lastly, there was his weight…

'You may think you're thin, but you still need to lose a few pounds to be at your optimum size.'

That really surprised Chris. He had been thin and gangly all his life – hence the *murungaru* nickname from the Safari Simbaz – and now he was being told he had to get even thinner and ganglier.

'Phew, that's a long list,' Chris thought. 'I've got a lot to learn if I'm going to make it as a top rider.'

But it wasn't all bad news.

'Don't worry,' John added as he saw the concern on Chris's face. 'All these things can be fixed and improved with hard work. The crucial thing is you're coping with our training programme and you are a good climber. You can't teach a sprinter to become a climber, no matter how hard you try.'

That made Chris feel better. The training with his new team had been harder than anything he'd known before, but it had not been *too* hard. His fanatical regime back in Jo'burg had meant his legs could cope with the long climbs and short sprint intervals they did every day.

Just as importantly, he was happy every time he got on the bike – like he always had been back home.

There were things he missed from Africa, of course. The European winter was cold. Make that, freezing. He missed those days riding in the blazing sun with Kinjah, the hot wind hitting their faces like a blowtorch. He kept in touch with his mum whenever he could and also gave regular reports to Robbie and Kinjah, who loved hearing how their star pupil was getting on.

'I'm learning how to become a proper rider,' he told Robbie over the phone. 'I try to take in something new each time I race. I've accepted that I will make mistakes – just hopefully not too many.'

'That's a good attitude, Chris. Keep that up and I'm sure you'll be winning races in no time for Konica Minolta.'

Robbie would be half-right. Chris did enjoy some success, but it came for the UCI development team who he was also riding for that season and were based in Switzerland.

He was selected to compete for the team in the Giro delle Regioni in Italy, a famous stage race for Under-23 riders.

'I hope I do better than my last Under-23 performance in the time trial in Salzburg,' Chris shuddered as he studied the course map, trying to block out memories of his collision with the marshal.

He drew a red circle around Stage 4, which had a big mountain finish. That would be his main target.

Once again, the gravity-defying hills brought the best out of Chris. As Stage 4 reached its finale, he was in a small pack of riders at the front of the race. He was enjoying how tough the climb was, and he liked it even more when he looked around to see his other competitors struggling.

'Okay. Time to go, Chris.'

He changed into a higher gear on his bike. That way, he would go faster if he put more force on his pedals. One final look at his rivals, then he stood up in his saddle. He put all the energy he could muster into his pedals and broke away – just as he had done in the Tour of Mauritius.

This time, however, he had company.

The Frenchman Cyril Gautier had spotted Chris's move and sped along with him.

Chris didn't panic. Instead he kept the pressure on.

'Let's see how he copes with the pace,' he thought.

With one kilometre remaining, Cyril was holding on, but only just. Chris could feel he was stronger.

He kept his cool. 'Bide your time. Don't rush too early.'

As soon as he spotted the finish line in the distance, he took off again. Cyril had nothing left. A gap opened up. Chris even had time to wave to the crowd as he crossed the line.

'Yessssssssssss!'

John Robertson, who was at the race with the South African Under-23 team, was one of the first to congratulate Chris at the finish.

'Great ride, Chris,' he said, shaking his hand. 'You've made history today.'

'What do you mean, John?'

'Don't you know? You are the first ever Kenyan to win a professional race in Europe.'

'No way.' Chris had no idea. He couldn't wait to tell his mum.

With that special victory in the bag, things got even better for Chris later that season when he won a stage in the Tour of Japan. He was starting to show that he had a promising future, and other teams were beginning to take notice.

As the end of the season approached, he received a phone call.

'Hi Chris, it's Robbie here. I'm interested in talking to you about your plans for next year.'

Chris scratched his head. 'Robbie? Who's Robbie?' he wondered. 'It's not Robbie Nilsen. I'd recognise his voice. Robbie… Robbie…'

Suddenly, it dawned on him. 'Robbie Hunter!' he shouted before quickly regaining his composure. 'Erm, sorry Robbie, it's a really, erm, bad line.'

Robbie was the greatest cyclist in South Africa's history and was now a leading rider for the Barloworld team. Robbie explained that his team had noticed Chris's climbing skills and would like him to join them for the new season.

'How does that sound?'

That sounded very good indeed. Barloworld were a well-known team and entered many of the big races, including – and this is what really excited Chris – the Tour de France. So he didn't bother looking around for any other teams and signed for Barloworld as soon as he could.

At twenty-two, Chris was older than most cyclists when they turned professional, but he was showing it had been worth the wait. He was proving he belonged at the elite level.

CHAPTER 13

HIGHS AND LOWS

After living in Kenya, South Africa, Belgium and Switzerland, Chris was used to moving around. Now he was on the move again. Joining Barloworld meant another new home in another new country.

'Welcome to Italy,' said Geraint Thomas in a distinctive Welsh accent. 'My name's Geraint, but everyone calls me G.'

'Pleased to meet to you, G. I'm Chris,' replied Barloworld's newest team member, offering a shivering hand to his teammate. The Italian winter seemed as bitterly cold as the rest of Europe.

'I'm afraid that just won't do,' said G.

Chris gave him a confused look.

'We've all got nicknames here, you see. Isn't that

right, Steve-o?' G shouted across the room to Steve Cummings. 'From now on, you're Froomey.'

Chris smiled. There was a lot to get used to in Italy. As well as a new name, there was another new language.

'Well, it can't be as hard as Swahili,' he told himself as he flicked through an Italian dictionary.

He was determined to have a good basic knowledge of Italian. It would help his communications with Barloworld's team boss Claudio Corti, as well as being really useful in day-to-day life – especially when it came to buying the right food in the supermarket.

Following John Robertson's advice, Chris had put a lot of effort into his diet and nutrition. If eating healthily meant improving his performance on the bike, then that's what he would have to do. Unfortunately, that meant sacrificing some of his favourite foods, and replacing them with some unusual dishes. He would get some very strange looks from the pasta-loving Italians when he sat down to eat his green lasagne.

'It's made of spinach,' Chris tried to explain to the puzzled locals. 'It's really good for you... and tastes okay too.'

The locals just shook their heads.

As different as life was in Italy, the winter period is always the same for a professional cyclist, wherever they might be. It was still all about the training.

While Chris enjoyed being part of a team, and sharing stories at the end of a day's ride with G and Robbie, he knew deep down that he worked best when he trained alone. Only then could he push his body to the very limit, just as Robbie Nilsen had taught him.

Although Chris would catch up with his teammates from time to time, he spent most of the winter alone, high up in the Italian hills with just his bike and an iPod for company. He drew up a punishing schedule and set about getting fitter than he'd ever been before.

Each day, there was one overriding thought driving him up every slope – the prospect of being selected for the Tour de France.

When spring arrived and the racing season started, it was a different story. Then it became all about teamwork. In professional cycling, the riders all work together for their team, rather than individual glory. The aim is to do as much as possible to help one of the stars of the team – like Robbie – win the stage or the race. For junior riders like Chris, that could mean anything from fetching bottles of water to cycling in front of Robbie to protect him from the wind – as well as from other cyclists. If Robbie's bike had a problem, Chris would jump off and give him his own bike – and would then have to wait until the Barloworld team car turned up with a replacement.

Chris understood that this was his main role and carried it out without any complaints. 'One day, I'd love to be a team leader,' he thought.

He did have some chances to go for a victory, however – particularly when any climbing was involved. The Intaka Tech World's View Challenge in South Africa was an early chance for Chris to test how well his winter training had gone, and a great opportunity to return to the country he knew so well.

On Stage 3, which involved a series of nasty-looking hills, the team gave Chris the green light to go for the win. The plan seemed to be working perfectly as Chris surged clear from the field on the final climb. As he entered the home straight, he relaxed and sat up in the saddle. He wanted to savour the moment and enjoy the win in front of the South African fans, but then...

WHOOSH!

Chris looked around in horror. The rest of the field had caught him before the finish. He tried to respond as they sped past him, but it was too late. He had thrown away a certain victory.

'I'm so embarrassed,' Chris said to Robbie afterwards, still shaking his head. Luckily, Robbie had been at the front of the chasing pack and had won the race for Barloworld, which saved Chris from a serious telling-off from Mr Corti.

'Don't be too hard on yourself, Froomey. You learned a valuable lesson today – the race isn't over until it's over.'

Chris managed to put that mishap behind him

and, back in Europe, enjoyed a run of strong results. As the Tour de France drew ever nearer, he started to wonder if he might be selected. Competition for places was very tough, Barloworld had lots of strong riders, and there were only nine spots available on the team.

But then a phone call from his brother Jeremy changed everything.

'Chris, I've got some bad news. It's Mum...'

After a short illness, Jane had passed away. It was a huge shock.

Suddenly, cycling wasn't important any more. A devastated Chris jumped on the first plane home.

He spent several weeks back in Kenya with his family. It was a very sad time, but there were lots of happy memories too. Jane had played such a big part in Chris's cycling dream when it was just the two of them in Nairobi. Over time, she had caught the cycling bug too, and long after Chris had left Kenya, she would regularly go and support the Safari Simbaz, bringing them welcome refreshments when they were out on the road.

Chris forgot all about cycling and Barloworld until his phone rang one day. It was Mr Corti.

'Chris, you're on the team for the Tour de France.'

Chris was stunned. The Tour? He hadn't thought about the Tour since he left Europe. He wasn't sure if he should go back so soon, but his brothers quickly reassured him.

'Get back there and follow your dream,' said Jeremy. 'That's exactly what Mum would have said.'

Chris nodded. He knew it was the right thing to do. It was time to go back to Europe.

He was going to ride in the Tour de France.

CHAPTER 14

THE TOUGHEST TEST

Two Colombians, two South Africans, two Italians, a Spaniard, an Australian and one Kenyan. The team who would represent Barloworld in the 2008 Tour de France was made up of riders from all over the globe. Some, like Robbie, were hugely experienced. Others, like Chris, were making their debut in the world's toughest cycling race.

Chris was a mixture of nerves and excitement as the team arrived in Brest.

'All set for the *Grand Départ* tomorrow, Froomey?' Robbie asked.

'Sorry, the what?'

'The *Grand Départ* is the name for the start of the Tour.'

'Oh, I see. Absolutely!'

There was so much for Chris to learn about this great race, and it hadn't even started yet. Even the map of the course looked daunting.

'You need a degree in geography to get your head around this,' Chris muttered as he traced the race from the start in Brest to the finish in Paris twenty-three days later.

The distances were enormous. They would ride all around France – plus a couple of days in Italy after crossing over the border. There were twenty-one different stages.

'What happens on the two days without stages?' Chris asked Robbie.

'They're rest days, Froomey. Trust me, if you're still in the race by then, you will be very grateful for them.'

Chris winced. It was a reminder of how hard the next three weeks would be. Of the 180 riders who started the Tour, a large number wouldn't make it to the finish. He was determined not to be one of them.

The next day, Chris was blown away by the sheer number of people who had gathered at the start.

Lines and lines of spectators were assembled at the side of the road, while there were more TV cameras, photographers and journalists than he had ever seen in his life.

'All these people just for this one race,' Chris whispered. He knew the Tour was a special event, but only now had he begun to realise how big it was.

He was also learning how to deal with the media. His participation had sparked some interest as he was the first ever Kenyan to compete in the Tour. Considering that the first Tour was held way back in 1903, it was a significant moment for Kenyan sport, and Chris was asked to do several interviews.

'It's very special and I hope I can make everyone who is watching proud,' he said.

His main focus, however, was not on the people back home, but the twenty-one stages that lay ahead.

Chris's primary task was to be a *domestique* – a rider who works for his team. The three teammates Chris was looking out for were Robbie, the sprinter Baden Cooke and their team leader Mauricio Soler.

Within a few hours of the start of the Tour, disaster

struck the Barloworld team. Mauricio crashed and broke his wrist. It was a huge blow to the team. He bravely continued for a couple more days before being forced to withdraw.

Chris, meanwhile, was fighting his own battles. He was just happy to make it to the end of each daily stage in one piece. The pace of the main group – the *peloton* as they were called – was quicker than he'd ever known before. *Domestiques* had to do whatever was required to help their team, even elbowing other riders or pushing them out of the way.

'What should I do?' Chris asked Robbie after one particularly bruising day's racing.

'Fight back, Froomey. It's dog-eat-dog out there.'

Chris quickly learned how to survive and resolved not to be bullied by any other riders.

After ten stages, he was beginning to settle into the race and even thinking he could possibly reach the finish, when he was told some devastating news. His Spanish teammate Moisés Dueñas had been disqualified from the race, having been caught cheating.

Chris was shell-shocked. He was distraught that one of his teammates would resort to such tactics. Cycling had a notorious history of people taking substances to improve their performances – even Ivan Basso, Chris's first ever hero from the 2002 Tour, had been caught cheating – but the sport was much cleaner these days. Lots of the cheats had been thrown out.

Chris strongly believed in fair play – the only way to get to the top was through hard work and effort. He was furious that people like Moisés were ruining his sport.

To make matters worse, rumours circulated that the whole Barloworld team might be disqualified as a result. That seemed hugely unfair to Chris. You couldn't punish the team for one person's actions.

The incident left a nasty taste in Chris's mouth, but luckily Barloworld were allowed to continue in the race – well, those who were left at any rate. By Stage 13, just four riders remained: Chris, Robbie, John-Lee Augustyn and Giampaolo Cheula.

'Will any of us make it to Paris?' Chris wondered.

With so few team members remaining, Chris

could put aside his *domestique* duties aside and test himself against the best in the mountains. Stage 17 was a day for the strongest climbers – a day that the *peloton* dreaded: they faced Alpe d'Huez, the most famous mountain in cycling.

At 1,850m, Alpe d'Huez was not the highest summit in the race, but it was certainly the hardest and most feared for riders, especially when they had already climbed two other colossal mountains earlier in the day.

The race would finish at Alpe d'Huez's summit. Chris felt a chill as he heard other riders talking about years gone by when they had cycled through snow to reach the finish. Despite all this, he was in confident mood as the *peloton* reached the foot of the mountain. His legs felt strong and he was ready for the challenge that faced him.

Within minutes, he was recalling John Robertson's warning a year earlier about the French Alps. John was right – it was extremely hard going – but he was surviving. As other riders fell away, Chris managed to stay with the leading pack.

It felt incredible to be in this position, but he couldn't get too carried away.

Chris gave himself a stern talking to: 'This isn't over yet.'

His legs started to ache with cramp. He soldiered on as best he could but eventually slipped back. The leaders were in the distance now; now, for Chris, the stage was a personal battle against the mountain.

The support of the crowds was unbelievable. Any time he slowed down or faltered, the fans would run alongside him and shout encouragement. Chris responded by speeding up – he didn't want to let them down.

At last, the finish was in sight. Chris had made it. He crossed the line in thirty-first place. He may not have won but he had conquered Alpe d'Huez.

Four days later, he was still standing as the race arrived in Paris. After 21 stages and 3,559 km, Chris had completed the Tour de France. He finished in 84th place, higher than his three surviving teammates.

Chris was exhausted. His whole body hurt. And he couldn't wait to do it all again.

CHAPTER 15

SKY'S THE LIMIT

'A rough, unpolished diamond with loads of
potential.'

So read the biography of Chris Froome on
the Team Sky website at the start of the 2010
season. Chris liked the 'potential' bit – 'rough' and
'unpolished' less so. But all in all he thought it was
probably a fair assessment.

He was one of twenty-six riders who had joined
the new team. Team Sky had been created by British
Cycling and its performance director Dave Brailsford,
who had spotted Chris all those years ago at the
Commonwealth Games. Dave was a huge name in
cycling these days. He had transformed the fortunes
of Great Britain's track cycling team, who won an

incredible seven gold medals at the 2008 Beijing Olympics. Now focusing on road cycling, his next aim was to win the Tour de France.

So when Dave got in touch at the end of the 2009 season to see if he was interested in joining the team, Chris was only too happy to accept his offer. Barloworld had fallen on tough times and would no longer be competing in 2010. It was the perfect time to move on to bigger and better things.

'Let's hope we can give you plenty more golden moments, Dave,' said Chris.

Team Sky had a very British feel. Chris learned that was a deliberate ploy by Dave. His aim was to produce the first British winner of the Tour de France within five years.

That was of particular interest to Chris. Although he had raced for Kenya in the past, he also held British citizenship. His parents had strong British roots and had given their children a typically British upbringing, with shepherd's pie and Sunday roasts both regular meals on the family table.

Chris had always felt British in his heart and,

while he was proud to represent Kenya, in 2008 he decided it was time to switch allegiance to Great Britain. Now he had the chance to fly the British flag for a British team.

A familiar face greeted Chris on day one of training.

'You can't stay away from us, Froomey!' Geraint Thomas greeted him with a big smile.

Chris grinned. 'Good to see you too, G.'

Also in the room were two other old Barloworld teammates, John-Lee Augustyn and Steve Cummings. There was a strong British presence with Pete Kennaugh, Ian Stannard and Ben Swift all on the roster, while the team leader was one of the greats of British cycling.

Bradley Wiggins had been a star of the track, winning medals at the previous three Olympic Games, including double gold in Beijing. Like Dave, he wanted to repeat that success on the road.

The team might have had a British flavour, but like Barloworld, it was based in Italy. Chris was relieved that for once he wouldn't have to learn yet another new language.

From their very first team meeting, Chris could tell that Team Sky meant business. They had prepared for everything. There were nutritionists, all kinds of different coaches, and actual proper physios. Other teams often used retired racers to give massages, with mixed results – Chris felt that sometimes his body would be sorer after the massage than before it!

The team bus, which would transport the riders to races, had to be seen to be believed. There were comfy chairs that turned into beds, TVs, showers, massage tables, fridges, even an office.

'This is nicer than my home,' Chris said to G.

'This *is* my home, Froomey,' G joked. 'Why bother paying rent when I've got everything I need right here?'

Joking aside, Chris was hugely encouraged by what he saw. Preparation was a key ingredient in a successful team, and Team Sky seemed to have all bases covered. All these factors, however small, could help Chris gain an advantage over riders in other teams.

Out on the road, the coaching staff offered plenty

of advice too. They taught Chris to sit in a different position on his bike, which meant he could use less energy while retaining the same speed.

'That will be really helpful on the long mountain stages when I need every last drop of energy in my body,' Chris thought.

They also gave him tips on how to race. Chris was taught when he should be at the back of the *peloton*, when he should sit in the middle of the pack and when he should be leading at the front.

There was so much to learn, but Chris was still only twenty-four. He had time on his side. For now, his main role in the team would be to work for others, like Brad.

'I understand I'm a junior rider compared to a lot of these guys, so I'm here to develop and learn,' he said to Dave when they talked excitedly about the season ahead.

Unfortunately, that excitement didn't last long. Chris's season was punctured by illness and injury, so he was unable to develop as much as he would have liked. He was chosen to ride in the Giro d'Italia, one of cycling's three biggest races, alongside the Tour de France and Vuelta a España. Together, the three races are called the 'Grand Tours'.

In the Giro d'Italia, Chris couldn't wait to get stuck into three weeks of hard work and high mountains, but his hopes of a strong performance were ruined early in the race when he injured his knee.

Most riders would have quit there and then, yet Chris was not most riders – and he certainly wasn't a quitter. The knee got worse and worse, but he refused to give in. He struggled on until Stage 19 when he was finally forced to call it a day.

'If you go on any further, you could do some permanent damage to your knee,' the doctor explained. 'It's not worth it, Chris. Go home and rest.'

The injury meant he had to miss the Tour de France and watch it on TV instead.

'Never again,' vowed Chris as he sat glumly at home. He wasn't a good indoors person at the best of times, but what choice did he have? To keep himself busy, he studied the best riders in the Tour and the tactics they used while racing. It made him feel better to know he was learning something, even if he wasn't out there with them.

Once the knee had finally healed, Chris showed everyone what he could do when fully fit, finishing fifth in the 2010 Commonwealth Games time trial in Delhi – this time for England, not Kenya. It was a reminder of his huge talent and a good way to sign off the year.

He was happy to see the back of a frustrating 2010. In 2011, he was determined that his talent would be turned into results for Team Sky.

The unpolished diamond was ready to realise his potential.

CHAPTER 16

RIDING INTO CONTENTION

Chris sat nervously at home, staring at his phone.

'Come on, why won't you ring? What's taking so long?'

The wait was excruciating.

Finally, the phone buzzed. It was his Team Sky coach, Bobby Julich.

'Froomey, we've had a chat and we've made a decision.'

'Come on, Bobby. Put me out of my misery.'

'It's good news – you've made the team for the Vuelta a España.'

Chris punched the air with joy.

'Thanks Bobby. I promise the team won't regret this decision. See you in Spain!'

After hanging up, he sat back down, took a deep breath, and let out an almighty scream.

'Yessssssssssssss!'

It was an enormous relief. Chris had started his 2011 season with such high hopes. He had decided to move – again – to Monaco, where he could focus better on his training programme. His new coach Bobby had taught him how to ride tactically:

'It's all about making the right decisions, Froomey. You can break away with 200 kilometres remaining and have your fifteen minutes of fame at the front before everyone catches you. Or you can wait for the right moment to make your move, and then cross the finish line first. I know which I'd prefer.'

Despite all this, Chris had failed to deliver when it really mattered – in the races. With fierce competition for places at Team Sky, he had missed selection for the Tour de France. The Vuelta a España – the third of cycling's three Grand Tours – was his last hope.

Team Sky could only take nine riders to Spain, and Chris had snuck into the team as their ninth and last rider. The Vuelta was a climber's dream. Of the twenty-one stages, nine involved mountains. Chris was determined to make the most of his opportunity.

'We believe Bradley Wiggins could become the first ever Briton to win the Vuelta – with your help,' Dave Brailsford told Chris. 'Your job is to get him safely up the mountains. Understood?'

Chris nodded. He made a promise to himself to be at Brad's side up each and every mountain. Come the end of the first week of the Vuelta, he had stuck to his word. The pair were quite literally side by side – Chris in 21st position, Brad next to him in 22nd.

The next day, Chris came crashing back to earth, ending up in a ditch after a collision in the *peloton*. Crashing was, unfortunately, part of life as a cyclist – a very painful part. Chris remembered John Robertson's warning about taking too many risks and made a mental note to learn how to stay out of trouble. But that would have to wait. All his focus right now was on Brad, not his own safety.

'We could be wearing the leader's red jersey by this evening,' Dave said enthusiastically at the team meeting before Stage 10. It was the day of the time trial – Brad's speciality.

Chris had always been strong at the time trial, too, and his legs were feeling really fresh that day. He poured every ounce of energy into pushing his pedals and flew along the course.

He posted a great time.

So great that he finished ahead of Brad.

So great that he became the new leader of the Vuelta!

Dave's prediction had come true – just not quite how he had imagined it.

Chris was stunned. Before he could gather his senses, he was dragged up onto the podium and presented with the red jersey worn by the race leader.

'This wasn't in the script,' he said to Bobby. 'What happens now?'

'Nothing has changed, Froomey. Brad is still our leader – go out there tomorrow and help get him up the mountain again.'

Chris understood. He was a junior rider and he had to help Brad to victory – regardless of the fact that he was leading. Besides, there was a long way still to go.

However, he was going to enjoy his time in the red jersey first.

It was a very special feeling out on the road next day. Fans screamed Chris's name all day long. Other riders cycled up to congratulate the new leader.

'Well done, Chris.'

'Brilliant ride yesterday, Froomey.'

'Red is definitely your colour!' joked Ian Stannard.

Chris happily accepted all the platitudes, but the climb soon wiped the smile off his face. He set a fierce pace up the mountain. The quicker he went, more and more riders dropped away, unable to keep up. All the time, Brad remained right behind his teammate.

Eventually, Chris had nothing left. He drifted back. He knew he would lose his lead, but he had done an incredible job for his team. Brad accelerated into the distance to become the new leader of the Vuelta.

'Amazing effort today, Froomey,' said Brad. 'I'm sorry that I have to take the red jersey off you.'

'Don't worry. I'm happy that Team Sky has still got it.'

For the next few days, it was business as usual as Chris did all he could to help his leader stay in front. But on Stage 14, the topsy-turvy race took yet another twist. On another brutal climb, Brad ran out of gas. Chris, as his loyal sidekick, stayed with his leader, trying everything he could to help him get to the top.

It was no use. Brad's tank was empty.

'You go ahead, Froomey,' he urged his teammate. 'I can't win the Vuelta, but you still can.'

Chris was caught in two minds. He didn't want to disobey team orders and leave his leader, but he didn't want to disobey his leader's orders either.

'Go on, Froomey, before it's too late.'

He knew Brad was right. He was feeling fresh. He had to go for it. He sped away up the hill.

Chris now became Team Sky's main hope for victory. With seven stages remaining, the Vuelta had suddenly become a two-horse race. Local favourite Juan José Cobo was the new leader, twenty seconds ahead of Chris. From now on, Team Sky would put all their efforts into delivering the win for Chris.

That night, Chris struggled to sleep as he thought about how far he'd come. 'Here I am. The boy from Nairobi. With a chance of winning a Grand Tour.'

His big chance came on Stage 17, where there were enough mountains to make his mouth water. To make the day even more special, both Noz and Jono had flown out to Spain to watch him in action.

Chris and Juan battled each other all the way up the final mountain. It was pandemonium in the crowd. Most fans were cheering on the Spaniard, but there was plenty of loud British support – particularly from Jono.

'Come on, bro. Keep going!'

As the finish line loomed, Chris put in one last burst and sprinted away from his rival. He had won his first stage in a Grand Tour – and Noz and Jono could not have been prouder.

The leader's red jersey remained agonisingly out of reach, however. The gap to Juan in the overall standings was now thirteen measly seconds. Not

much longer than it takes Usain Bolt to run the
100 m.

In the last four stages, Chris tried everything he
could to overturn the lead, but all to no avail. He
finished second overall, with Brad in third place.

He was understandably disappointed not to win,
but Noz quickly cheered him up.

'What a great effort, son. There's absolutely no
shame in finishing second. Did you know that is the
closest a British rider has ever come to winning a
Grand Tour?'

'Really?'

'I bet Team Sky are glad they picked you now.'

CHAPTER 17

DOMESTIQUE DUTY

'I've missed this,' Chris said to his teammate Richie Porte, with a big grin on his face. 'It's good to be back.'

The two Team Sky riders were waiting at the start of the ninety-ninth edition of the Tour de France. It was 2012, four long years since Chris had last taken part in the great race.

'You've been away so long I'm surprised you managed to find the start line!' Richie said to him.

Like a typical Australian, Richie was always cracking gags at his mate's expense. Not that Chris minded at all; it was healthy not to think about cycling all day every day – and he could certainly take the mickey out of Richie too if his friend got too cocky.

Richie had joined Team Sky for the 2012 season and the pair had quickly forged a strong friendship, so much so that they shared a room together during races. Like Chris, Richie was a great climber and would be a key part of the team over the next three weeks.

After his incredible performance at the Vuelta a España, Chris had hoped that 2012 might be the year when he could go for glory in the Tour de France, but cycling wasn't that simple. There was a pecking order in place, and Bradley Wiggins was still the main man at Team Sky. He had been in top form all season, winning races here, there and everywhere. So it came as no surprise to Chris when Dave Brailsford decided that Brad would be their main man in France – and the other eight riders would help him do it. Chris would be a *domestique* again.

'Froomey, you're our best climber. You'll be Brad's right-hand man in the mountains,' Dave said. 'As second in command, if something goes wrong for Brad, you'll be ready to lead the team.'

Chris nodded. He understood Dave's thinking. The

team's best chance of victory was if they all worked together for one rider, especially as there were so many other top-quality cyclists in the race.

'We're up against the defending champion Cadel Evans and the great Italian, Vincenzo Nibali – to name just two,' he said to Richie. 'This is going to be really tough.'

'We'll do everything we can to help Brad finish first,' Richie replied.

The Tour started well for Team Sky and just got better and better. On Stage 2, Mark Cavendish, Chris's Great Britain teammate, sprinted to victory.

'How quick was Cav today? He sped past us in a blur,' said Chris.

'That's why they call him the "Manx Missile",' Richie laughed.

Come Stage 7, it was Chris's turn. It was the first big mountain stage of the race. The Team Sky plan worked perfectly. First, Bernie Eisel led them up the mountain, then – when he had run out of energy – Mick Rogers took over. One by one, other riders fell back. The pace was too hot.

It got even hotter after Richie took over from Mick and, when he had nothing left, it was Chris's job to give his all and get Brad safely to within 1 km of the finish. Except, on this occasion, as the final 500 m approached, Chris was still at the front. He had energy to burn and only Brad and Cadel left for company.

'I feel really fresh. I can win this,' Chris thought. He looked around. Brad was safe now, the finish was in sight. He took a deep breath and sprinted for the line.

Victory!

Chris was too strong. He had won his first stage at the Tour, by two seconds.

Even better, Brad became the new race leader. He would wear the yellow jersey, the most famous shirt in cycling.

A couple of days later, Brad increased his lead after winning the time trial, just ahead of Chris, before the race returned to the mountains. On Stage 11, Team Sky dealt another hammer blow to their rivals' hopes with some ferocious riding. Once again, Chris was in fine form and enjoying the suffering. He decided to push even harder.

Hang on a minute. There was someone missing.

He looked around to see Brad struggling in the distance.

Alarm bells started ringing.

The pace was too quick.

He had left his leader behind.

Chris immediately slowed down and let Brad catch him up again. They stayed together until the finish. Disaster averted. Phew.

Despite that scare, it was a very good day for the team. Chris was no longer just the second man at Sky, he had moved into second place in the whole race.

In the interviews afterwards, though, some reporters asked if he should have left Brad and gone for the yellow jersey himself, but Chris was having none of it.

'Brad is our leader and my main job is to ride for Brad,' he said.

Of course, he would have loved to wear the

yellow jersey, but that particular dream was on hold this year. Chris was a loyal teammate, and helping Brad win the Tour was all that mattered right now.

Chris's girlfriend Michelle showed her support for him on Twitter: 'If you want loyalty, get a Froome dog!'

'Great, thanks Michelle,' Chris grinned as he read the message that the whole world could see. 'Another nickname to add to the list.'

As the Tour reached its last few days, the result was never in doubt. There was one time trial to come, then the final stage. Brad was the best in the business at the time trial and won the stage, further increasing his lead. The next day, as the riders cycled towards the grand finale in Paris, Brad took up his now very familiar position alongside Chris.

'Your time will come, Froomey. Next year we'll be supporting you.'

Chris smiled. That sounded like a very good plan.

There was a special ceremony in Paris after the race ended. Brad stood on the top spot of the podium. Chris was next to him – he finished in second place, three minutes, twenty-one seconds behind. They were joined by Vincenzo Nibali in third place, who was a further three minutes behind.

Dave couldn't stop smiling. Team Sky had been totally dominant, and Brad was the first ever Briton to win the Tour – three years ahead of Dave's schedule!

Chris was also delighted but he knew he would never be 100 per cent happy until *he* was standing on the top of the podium. The past three weeks had only made him hungrier than ever to win the Tour.

He needed a rest, but he had no time to relax. In six days, he would be racing in the London Olympics.

CHAPTER 18

LONDON CALLING

'We love you, Brad.'

'Go on, Froomey.'

'Unleash the Manx Missile.'

'GB, GB, GB!'

Chris stared in wonder at the spectators as he cycled past. Even if he had had time to stop, there were far too many of them to count. Everyone was screaming their support for Chris, Brad, Cav and the British team.

'I thought the Tour de France was crazy,' he shouted to Cav over the cheers. 'This is ten times louder.'

'Sorry, Froomey, what did you say?'

Even though he was sweating from all the pedalling, Chris had goosebumps. It was an amazing feeling. He had loved competing for Kenya but had always wanted to represent Great Britain. And now here he was riding for Team GB in the men's road race in their home Olympic Games in London.

It was the first day of the Olympics and the British team were aiming to get the Games off to the best possible start and win gold. Their best hope lay with Cav, the team's speedy sprinter.

'The race finishes on The Mall in central London, right next to Buckingham Palace,' Chris said to Cav. 'Our plan is to put you in a position where you can sprint for gold on the final straight.'

'Let's hope the Queen will be watching!' Cav joked.

Unfortunately, as Chris had learned many times over the past few years, things didn't go to plan. Cav was too far back to catch the leaders when the race reached its climax, and it was won by Alexander Vinokourov from Kazakhstan.

Chris felt bad – for Cav and for all the fans.

'Sorry, Cav, I would have loved nothing more than for you to win gold.'

'There's no need to apologise, Froomey. We all

tried our best, but it wasn't to be. Make sure you win a medal for GB in the time trial.'

The time trial? Of course! Amid all the excitement, Chris had forgotten that he had another race in four days – and this time, he wouldn't be riding for his teammates, but for himself.

In professional cycling, there are good climbers, good sprinters and good time triallers. But it's very rare for a cyclist to be an expert at more than one of these.

Chris was an exception. One of the strongest climbers in the world, he was also brilliant at racing against the clock in the time trial. He fancied his chances of sneaking a medal, but faced extremely tough competition. There was Tony Martin, the reigning time trial world champion from Germany. There was Fabian Cancellara, the four-time world time trial winner from Italy. And of course, there was Brad who had won both time trials at the recent Tour de France.

Chris gulped. He would need the race of his life to have any hope of a medal.

The course was 44 km long and started and ended at the famous Hampton Court Palace. If anything,

Chris thought even more fans had come out to watch that day than at the road race. They were certainly just as loud.

'Come on, Froomey.'

'Great ride, Chris.'

'Go for gold, Froome dog!'

The crowd's support made him pedal harder. At the halfway stage of the time trial, the GB team told Chris over the radio – which was hooked up to his ear – that he was in contention for a medal.

So Chris pushed even harder. The pain was hard to take, even by his standards, but he wouldn't back down. He was determined to win a medal for all the loyal fans.

It was an enormous relief when the finish line was in sight.

'One last push, Chris,' he told himself.

He powered to the line and stopped the clock at 51 minutes, 47 seconds.

The good news was Chris was in first place.

The bad news was there were still six more riders to come.

One … two … three … more riders finished. Chris was ahead of all of them. He then moved down to second place after Tony recorded a time 26 seconds faster.

Second quickly became third, as Brad scorched around the final corner to post a stunning time of 50 minutes, 39 seconds.

There was one more rider to come. Fabian Cancellara, arguably the greatest time trialler in history. Could Chris hang on for a medal?

He was so nervous he could barely watch. Time seemed to stand still as he stared at the clock.

Tick, tock, tick, tock. He counted every second go past.

Finally, Fabian came into view. He charged towards the finish line, but it wasn't enough. He couldn't beat Chris's time.

The crowd went mad. Gold for Brad and bronze for Chris. What a result for Team GB.

Chris raised both arms in the air. He wanted to win every race he entered but finishing third in such a high-quality field felt like a victory in its own right.

Soon afterwards, he was on the podium alongside Brad again – just like at the Tour – to collect his medal. It was a very special moment and when the British National Anthem was played, Chris welled up with pride.

It had been an unforgettable day – not just for Chris, but for the whole British team. That morning, Helen Glover and Heather Stanning had won Team GB's first gold of the Games on the rowing lake, then the men's rowing eight had followed up with a bronze. Later, swimmer Michael Jamieson bagged a silver in the pool.

From that point on, Britain did not look back. Every day brought more medals. Cycling was particularly successful, with the Brits winning an astonishing seven golds on the track, including a victory for Geraint Thomas in the team pursuit. Chris knew G would have plenty to say about that result when they met up again with Team Sky!

Team GB finished the Games with twenty-nine gold medals and sixty-five medals in all. And Chris was so proud to have played his part in his country's success.

CHAPTER 19

THE MAIN MAN

'Tomorrow Chris will begin his bid for victory in the Tour de France,' said Dave Brailsford.

Everyone in the room cheered and thumped the table excitedly. Chris smiled as he looked around the room at his teammates.

There was Geraint Thomas, his larger-than-life Welsh friend whom he had known since their time at Barloworld. There was Ian Stannard and Pete Kennaugh, two trusty allies from Team GB, and there was Richie – the best sidekick of all.

All eight teammates would help him in his bid to win the Tour, and he couldn't wish for a better group of teammates.

The mood might have been relaxed in the Team Sky

meeting room as they made their final preparations, but in a few hours no one would be laughing.

Chris now faced the biggest three weeks of his life.

It had been an easy decision for Team Sky to choose Chris as their leader. If his performances at the Vuelta a España and 2012 Tour showed he had the ability, his form in the first half of 2013 proved that ability beyond doubt. While Bradley Wiggins was struggling with injury and illness, Chris was a man on a mission.

Tour of Oman? Win.

Critérium International? Same again.

Tour de Romandie? Another victory.

Critérium du Dauphiné? You guessed it.

Yet all those races paled into insignificance compared with the three-week Tour. The 2013 event would be even more special than normal – it was the one hundredth edition of the famous race. And all the best riders in the world were desperate to win it.

'We'll have to watch the Colombian, Nairo Quintana, in the mountains,' said Richie. 'He's the best climber in the world.'

'Alberto Contador will fancy his chances too. He's already won the Tour twice,' G said.

'And don't forget his fellow Spaniards Alejandro Valverde and Joaquim Rodríguez,' added Pete. 'They're a massive threat.'

Chris listened to all the comments, then had his say. 'You're right – we're up against some really good riders, but first and foremost we need to concentrate on what we're doing at Team Sky, and not worry about other people. I strongly believe we've got the best team. Let's go out there tomorrow and get off to the best possible start.'

If only it was that simple.

At the start of each day on the Tour, the riders cycle through a neutral zone on their way to the official start line. It's a gentle ride, with no one travelling at much more than 20 km/h.

On the first stage, there was a lot of tension and nervous energy among the riders. Chris noticed it immediately.

'I don't want to get stuck in the pack. I'm going

to head to the front,' he told Richie as he began to accelerate.

As he weaved past other riders, there was suddenly a sharp bend in the road. Chris turned, but it was too late. He headed off course … and straight into a concrete barrier.

CRASH!

His bike buckled under the impact and he fell off. Fortunately, he was fine, although his bike wasn't. He would need a replacement.

'How embarrassing,' Chris thought as he sheepishly waved over the team car. 'The race hasn't even started and I'm already onto my second bike. And just when I thought I'd got rid of the "Crash Froome" nickname!'

Ultimately, there was no serious harm done, but that wasn't the end of the day's mishaps. As the riders approached the finale, the bus of the Orica-GreenEdge team got stuck under the banner signalling the end of the race. So the official finish line had to be moved back, and there was promptly a massive crash in the home straight.

Chris managed to steer clear of the pile-up but G wasn't so lucky. He was catapulted off his bike and landed badly. They found out later he had broken his pelvis.

'Are you okay to continue?' Chris asked.

'It'll take more than a few broken bones to stop me, Froomey. They build us tough in Wales!'

G's determination to carry on inspired the whole team.

By the time they arrived at Stage 8, Chris was licking his lips. There were 195 km in all – and many of them hilly! His teammates rose to the challenge – quite literally. The Belarusian Vasil Kiryienka led the charge up the final mountain. He handed over to Pete who continued the relentless pace. Then it was Richie's turn to drive another nail in their rivals' coffins. Joaquim couldn't handle the pace, nor could 2011 champion Cadel Evans.

With 5 km to go, Chris pounced. His rivals had been worn out by Team Sky and no one could respond.

After Chris crossed the line to win the stage, it was

fifty-one seconds until another rider appeared. And even better, that rider was Richie!

Team Sky had dealt a crushing blow to their opponents and Chris was now the new race leader. He was lost for words as he was handed the yellow jersey in the ceremony after the race. This was something he had dreamed about for a long, long time.

Chris quickly learned that, as the wearer of the yellow jersey, he had lots of commitments and couldn't just jump on the Sky bus like normal. As well as the ceremony, there were interviews, interviews and more interviews.

His main message was: 'I've got the yellow jersey and if anyone else wants it, they're going to have to wrestle it off me.'

Fighting talk!

A few days later, Chris extended his overall lead by two minutes after a strong time trial.

'You're doing brilliantly, Froomey,' Dave said that evening. 'But remember, there's a long way to go – and you never know what this race can throw at you.'

Chris nodded. After waiting so long for his chance, he would never take anything for granted, especially with so many high-class opponents wanting to take his jersey.

On Stage 13, his rivals bit back. Alberto Contador and Dutchman Bauke Mollema made a break when no one expected it. Team Sky were caught napping and, try as they might, could not reel them in.

While Chris was downcast at the end of the stage, Richie had some wise words to share: 'Everyone has a bad day in the Tour, mate. It's a matter of making sure you limit your losses when you have one.'

It was great advice. It wasn't a catastrophe, but Chris could ill-afford another bad day. His lead over Bauke had been significantly cut to two minutes, twenty-two seconds.

The Tour was far from over.

CHAPTER 20

TOUR DE FORCE

Chris's eyes were fixed on the road beneath him. All he could focus on was moving one pedal after the other. Each push required an enormous effort. His bike crept up the mountain.

Eventually, he looked up. In the distance, about thirty metres up the road, he could see the navy blue shirt of the Colombian, Nairo Quintana. Then he checked behind him.

'Yep, Alberto's still there.' The Spanish rider Alberto Contador was practically glued to his wheel.

'So, just the three of us left,' Chris said to himself. 'Oh, and thousands upon thousands of fans!'

Spectators lined both sides of the road: one, two, three rows deep. They were so close that Chris could reach out and high-five them – not that he had the energy.

It was Stage 15 and the Tour de France had arrived at Mont Ventoux, the toughest climb of the whole race.

'Why do they call it the "Bald Mountain"?' Chris had asked Geraint Thomas earlier in the day.

'Probably because it makes you tear your hair out!' G replied with a chuckle.

G and the rest of Chris's teammates were no longer alongside him on the Bald Mountain. They had each put in huge efforts to help him before falling away from the leading pack, completely drained.

'If you want to win the Tour, it's up to you and you alone,' Chris told himself.

With that thought fresh in his mind, he propelled his bike up the mountain and away from Alberto. The Spaniard could not respond.

'One down, one to go.'

Slowly but surely, Chris was catching up with Nairo – like a fisherman reeling in a prized catch. As soon as he reached him, Chris accelerated again. But the Colombian was onto him in a flash.

Chris kept pushing, trying to wear down his rival, but Nairo stuck to him like a magnet. The cries from the crowd grew ever louder as the finish drew nearer.

Suddenly, there was an almighty cheer. Chris spun around.

Nairo was gone!

The crowd were going wlld. The pain was excruciating but Chris knew he must not slow down now.

'Remember those days back in Jo'burg,' he told himself. 'Never give in.'

Finally, the finish appeared, putting an end to his suffering. He punched the air as he crossed the line, having just enough energy to lift his arm from the handlebar.

It was his greatest ever win.

There was still a week to go, and plenty more mountains to climb, but Chris now had one hand on the yellow jersey. His overall lead was more than four minutes and, just as importantly, he had shown his rivals he was practically unbeatable.

Chris refused to get carried away, though. 'Let's just take it one stage at a time,' he told his teammates that evening.

Over the next week, the team focused on defending Chris's lead. Any time a rival attacked, they would chase him down. No one could cut the gap. For good measure, Chris even won the time trial on Stage 17 to increase his advantage.

After Stage 20, he led by over five minutes. There was just one more stage to go – and that was the processional stage to the finish line in Paris, where it was tradition not to attack the yellow jersey.

Chris was the champion in waiting – barring any last-minute disasters.

'Don't worry, mate,' Richie said in their hotel room that evening. 'All you need to do is get to the finish line in one piece and you'll be the champion.'

But Chris couldn't sleep – and not just because of Richie's snoring! He was 133.5 km away from achieving his dream.

He thought back to Kinjah and all those days riding together through the hills in the blazing sun.

He thought back to Jo'burg, and the long rides on his bike on his own, when he refused to take the easy option and go home, and instead climbed one more hill.

He thought back to all the junior competitions in South Africa, when Noz had got up at the crack of dawn to drive him to another race.

And he thought about his mum. She would have been so proud to see him now.

It was an incredible feeling riding into Paris the next day. Lots of riders came up to Chris to offer their congratulations. It seemed like half of Britain had made the trip to France to cheer him on; there were hundreds of Union flags flying in the air.

Chris savoured every second as they cycled around Paris's famous Champs-Élysées to finish the race. At the end, the Team Sky riders crossed the line together, arm in arm.

'Well done, Froomey,' they all shouted.

'This is a victory for the whole team, boys,' Chris replied.

After 83 hours, 56 minutes and 40 seconds, he had finally finished the race.

Chris was the Tour de France champion!

There were plenty of recognisable faces waiting to greet him. He disappeared into a sea of hugs from – among others – his brother Jeremy, his girlfriend Michelle, and Matt Beckett, his old training partner from the school days at St John's. They had all played a part in helping him get here.

All that was left to do was the official ceremony and a victory speech. As darkness fell in Paris, Chris – shining brightly in his yellow jersey – leapt onto the top step of the podium. It felt so much sweeter than one year earlier.

Chris thanked his teammates and loved ones for all their support, but he wanted to dedicate his win to one special person above all:

'Without Mum's encouragement to follow my dreams, I'd probably be at home watching this event on TV. It's a great shame she never got to come and see the Tour, but I'm sure she'd be extremely proud if she were here tonight.'

CHAPTER 21

CRASHING BACK TO EARTH

'Watch out!' Chris cried out. But it was too late.

The rider swerved into his path.

The next thing Chris knew he was skidding across the road – without his bike. He looked up to see the *peloton* flying past at a frightening speed.

'Please don't ride over me,' he thought.

When they had safely passed, he pushed himself up.

'Aaarrrggghhh.' A sharp pain in his wrist.

He started walking back to his bike.

'Aaarrrggghhh.' His hip really hurt too.

'Are you okay to continue, Froomey?' Dave Brailsford asked over the Team Sky radio.

There was no reply. Chris was already back on his bike and heading off into the distance.

'There's my answer,' Dave smiled, but he was worried about his team leader.

With so many cyclists riding so quickly, one mistake can spell disaster in a race. It's even worse in the first week of the Tour de France, when there are many more riders and even less room to move. Some of the cyclists are inexperienced and haven't ridden in such a big race before, which makes accidents more likely – and that is exactly what happened to Chris on Stage 4 when another competitor knocked him off his bike.

Luckily, his Sky teammates were on hand to help him catch up with the rest of the *peloton*. He bravely finished the stage without any further drama, but he was in a lot of pain and went to see the doctor that evening.

'It's bad news, I'm afraid,' the doctor said.

Chris's heart sank.

'It looks like you've fractured your wrist and fractured your hand too. And your hip and elbow are both badly bruised.'

Chris sat in silence for a few seconds as he took in the news.

'Am I okay to continue the race?'

The doctor was astonished. 'You want to continue riding?'

Chris managed a smile. 'Clearly, you don't know me very well!'

After winning the 2013 Tour, he was desperate to become the first British rider to successfully defend his title in 2014 – and he wasn't prepared to give up on his dream just yet.

It was crushing news, though, and a far cry from the glorious scenes a few days earlier when the Tour had officially started in Leeds.

'They're calling this the Tour de Yorkshire,' Chris joked with Richie as he waved to the fans. The British public had come out in their thousands to show their support, particularly for the Team GB riders. It was a carnival atmosphere.

In the days leading up to the race, Chris had even been asked to do his own special ride to mark the fact that the Tour de France was starting in England.

'We know you're an expert at riding up

mountains. How do you feel about riding under the sea?' the organisers asked him.

'That sounds… impossible,' Chris replied with a frown.

'Not when you're cycling through the Channel Tunnel!'

So Chris became the first ever cyclist to ride in the tunnel – from Folkestone in the south of England to Calais in northern France. He was determined to set a fast time too and completed the journey in fifty-five minutes – quicker than a ferry crossing!

In all, there were three stages in England, with the third day finishing in London. Chris was well placed in fifth overall, just two seconds off the lead, but then took a tumble on Stage 4, and his world came crashing down.

His mood got even worse when he hobbled to the window and drew back the curtains on the morning of Stage 5.

'Oh no, rain,' he said to Richie gloomily.

'Don't worry, mate. The whole team will be by your side to help you get through today.'

There was only so much his teammates could do. If it wasn't hard enough riding in the world's toughest race with a broken wrist and hand, on a wet and slippery road it became nigh on impossible for Chris to control his bike.

Within half an hour of the stage starting, he crashed again. The pain was almost unbearable, but he was determined not to give up.

'Froomey, are you sure you want to carry on?' Dave asked.

Chris gritted his teeth and got back in the saddle.

But it was no use. Shortly afterwards, he lost control of his bike and fell again. This time, he knew his body wasn't going to let him continue.

As the Team Sky car pulled up, Chris opened the door and got inside. His Tour de France campaign was over.

Later that day, he made a statement.

'Devastated to have to withdraw from this year's Tour de France. Injured wrist and tough conditions made controlling my bike near to impossible. Thanks to the team and support staff for trying to get me through today.'

It was the biggest disappointment of his career. As everyone knew, Chris was not a quitter, but on this occasion he had no choice.

'It was the right decision, Froomey,' Dave said. 'If you'd have kept going, there would have been a real risk that you could have done some permanent damage to your body. Now you need to rest, then focus on coming back stronger than ever for next year's Tour.'

Chris nodded as he made a silent vow to himself. He would come back fitter and stronger than anyone could imagine.

CHAPTER 22

MAKING HISTORY

'Listen up, everyone. Here's the plan. We're going to win the Tour de France in the first week.'

Chris's words were met by a room of blank faces. Eventually, Geraint Thomas piped up.

'Erm, Froomey, have you forgotten the Tour lasts for three weeks?'

Chris chuckled. 'No, G, I'm well aware of that! But looking at the quality of the other teams and riders in this year's race, it's going to be closer than ever. If we can get an early lead in the first week, then that might prove crucial come Paris. Every second counts.'

It was a great plan. Traditionally, the winner of the Tour was decided in the second and third weeks when the race entered the mountains. But if Team Sky could spring a surprise on their rivals when they were least expecting it on the flat stages in the first week, those tactics could be the secret to winning the race.

Winning the race had been at the centre of Chris's thoughts morning, day and night ever since he was forced to withdraw from the 2014 Tour. Of course, there had been times when he'd thought about other things: his wedding to Michelle, for instance, or other races, as when he had bounced back from injury to finish second in the Vuelta a again. Even so, the Tour always occupied a special spot in his brain.

Team Sky had an even stronger British feel in 2015, with Chris joined by G, Pete Kennaugh, Ian Stannard and debutant Luke Rowe. Richie was still there too, flying the flag for Australia.

'You can have all the Brits you want, Froomey,' he joked, 'but when you're halfway up a mountain, gasping for air, you'll be crying out for an Aussie to help you.'

Team Sky quickly set about putting Chris's plan into action.

On Stage 2, Chris took advantage of the strong winds to join a breakaway group. He finished eighty-eight seconds ahead of defending champion Vincenzo Nibali and Nairo Quintana.

On Stage 3, he was at it again, gaining precious seconds on Vincenzo, Nairo and Alberto Contador too. By the end of the day, he was already putting on the yellow jersey as the race leader.

'This is going even better than I'd imagined!' Chris told Richie that evening.

'Long way to go yet, mate.'

As if to prove Richie's point, Tony Martin took the yellow jersey the very next day. Tony was not a big threat as the overall race winner, but it showed how tight the race would be.

By Stage 7, Chris was leading the way once more. The previous day, Tony had crashed just before the finish and was unable to continue the race. Chris, however, refused to wear the yellow jersey at the start of Stage 7, as he felt it wasn't the right thing to do when another rider had been injured.

'That's really sporting of you, Chris,' said Tony. 'Good luck for the rest of the race.'

'Thanks, Tony. I know exactly how tough it is to withdraw from the Tour with injury. Get well soon.'

The first week had gone perfectly to plan. There were many twists and turns ahead but Chris had gained valuable seconds over all his key rivals.

And now that he was in front again, he was even more determined not to relinquish the lead.

He was 12 seconds ahead, but crucially he had opened up a gap of 1 minute, 59 seconds on Nairo, who looked like his main threat in the mountains.

'So, what's your new plan now that week one is over?' Richie asked.

Chris grinned. 'To get an even bigger lead in the mountains.'

The very next day, he set about doing exactly that. Faced with a 15 km climb to finish Stage 10, Chris sprinted away from his rivals halfway up the mountain. He still had 6.5 km to go on his own, but he was perfectly happy in his own company. He had done it his whole career – in the hills outside Jo'burg, training in Italy without his Team Sky mates, and even in Salzburg when he went to the junior world championships on his own to represent Kenya!

He settled into a rhythm he was comfortable with and before long all the chasing pack could see was a little yellow dot in the distance.

Chris won the stage but, as much as he enjoyed individual victories, there was something even more important – his lead over Nairo was up to 3 minutes, 9 seconds.

'Great ride, Froomey,' G said at the finish. 'It's nearly in the bag now.'

'We might need every one of those seconds, G. Nairo always fights back.'

For the next eight stages, that was exactly how it remained. The Colombian couldn't eat into the three-minute advantage.

'What did I tell you, Froomey? It's in the bag now,' said G again, giving his teammate a friendly thump on the back.

But Chris's reply remained the same. 'Nairo always fights back.'

On Stage 19, his prediction came true. Nairo attacked on the last climb of the day, and for once Chris's legs couldn't respond. His lead was down to 2 minutes, 38 seconds, with one competitive stage to go before the procession into Paris.

Stage 20 was a repeat of the previous day from Nairo. Attack, attack, attack until he broke clear up the final mountain of the Tour – the dreaded Alpe d'Huez,

Chris knew he wouldn't catch the Colombian. It was no longer a race to win the stage. It was now a race against the clock.

Could he protect his overall lead?

'Every second counts,' he told himself while pedalling as hard as he could.

His legs were heavy, his lungs were bursting, everything hurt! But he had to keep going – he needed to save as much time as possible. It was going to be so close.

As he drove towards the finish line, Chris glanced up at the clock.

He had done it – just! His overall lead had been sliced by more than half, but he still held a seventy-two-second advantage over Nairo.

Chris had made history as the first Briton ever to win the Tour twice.

And without that precious lead in the first week, he would have ended up in second place.

The next day, as the Team Sky riders crossed the finish line together in Paris, once again all in a row, Chris let out a whoop of joy.

'I told you every second counts!'

CHAPTER 23

TOP OF THE WORLD

'What's he doing?'

'Is he crazy?'

'Where's his bike?'

No one had ever seen anything like it before in the cycling world. Chris, the leader of the Tour de France, was running up Mont Ventoux!

On both sides of the road, fans were cheering wildly for the man in the yellow jersey. His bike lay fifty metres back on the road, a tangled mess.

Chris was just as surprised as everyone else. He had been cycling up the mountain with two other riders – Richie Porte, who for the 2016 season had left Team Sky to join BMC Racing as their team leader, and Bauke Mollema. Suddenly, the TV motorbike directly in front of them stopped and Richie crashed into the back of it.

And Bauke crashed into Richie.

And Chris crashed into Bauke.

And another motorbike crashed into Chris.

Chris's bike was ruined. While the other two riders were able to continue up Mont Ventoux, Chris was left without a bike – and the Team Sky car that had a replacement bike was nowhere to be seen.

He decided to take matters into his own hands.

'Desperate times take desperate measures. I'm not waiting around any longer,' he said to himself. And he started to jog.

The crowd went mad.

Eventually, to Chris's enormous relief, a car pulled up and he jumped on a new bike. 'That feels much more familiar,' he thought as he cycled the remaining short distance to the finish.

At the end of the stage, the race organisers made the sensible decision to give all three riders the same time, which meant Chris kept his overall lead.

That evening, there was only one topic of conversation at the Team Sky hotel.

'Perhaps next year Chris will run the Paris Marathon,' said Dave Brailsford.

'Watch out, Mo Farah. Froomey's after you!' G chuckled.

Chris grinned at all the jokes, but it was no laughing matter for his rivals. Once again, Chris had shown he would do whatever it took to win the Tour – with or without a bike. The 2016 race was following a similar pattern to 2013 and 2015. Chris was unstoppable.

He had made his first decisive move on Stage 8. On this occasion, he didn't gain time going uphill as so often happened – but going downhill instead! He had remembered all the past advice from his old Konica Minolta team boss John Robertson. He still liked to fly down the hills at top speed, but he no longer took stupid risks.

Chris caught everyone napping at the top of the final climb. As everyone reached the summit and took a quick breather before the descent, he sped up and charged down the other side. He had opened up a fifty-metre lead before anyone could react.

The gamble paid off. Chris won the stage and, with it, the leader's yellow jersey. He held onto the yellow jersey for the remainder of the race.

By the time they arrived in Paris for the processional stage to the finish, Chris's overall lead was more than four minutes. His final time was 89 hours, 4 minutes and 48 seconds – including a couple of minutes of running!

It was his third Tour victory in four years. An incredible achievement.

Making the celebrations even more special was the fact that there was a new face waiting in Paris to see him crowned champion – his baby son Kellan.

'It's an absolutely amazing feeling. It feels like a privilege to be in this position,' Chris said at the end of the race.

The icing on the cake came a few weeks later, at the Olympic Games in Rio de Janeiro, when he added a bronze medal in the time trial to the one he had won in London four years earlier.

Chris was on top of the cycling world. He had fulfilled his dream of winning the Tour de France, the sport's greatest race – not once, but three times. Yet there was still so much more he wanted to achieve. A fourth Tour de France win, for starters – only four men had ever done that before. Victory in a Grand Tour in Italy or Spain and an Olympic gold in Tokyo 2020 were also in his sights.

For Chris Froome, the greatest road cyclist in British history, there was always a new challenge around the next corner.

CHRIS FROOME HONOURS

Tour de France

★ 2013, 2015, 2016

Olympic Games

★ Time trial: bronze (2012, 2016)

World Championships

★ Team time trial: bronze (2013)

Critérium du Dauphiné

★ 2013, 2015, 2016

Herald Sun Tour
★ 2016

Vuelta a Andalucia
★ 2015

Tour de Romandie
★ 2013, 2014

Tour of Oman
★ 2013, 2014

Critérium International
★ 2013

Tour of Mauritius
★ 2006

Turn the page for a sneak preview of
another brilliant sporting story by
John Murray. . .

USAIN BOLT

Available now!

978 1 78606 467 7

CHAPTER 1

THE GREATEST

Usain Bolt stood on the track and waited. He had just 100 metres left to run in his Olympic career. After three Olympic Games and a sackful of medals and memorable moments, it had all come down to this final moment.

He looked around the magnificent Olympic Stadium in Rio de Janeiro. Sixty thousand fans were packed into the venue, ready to watch the final of the 4x100m relay. Many of them were cheering his name.

'We love you, Usain.'

'Let's make it three out of three, Usain.'

'I want to see the Lightning Bolt!'

He had first burst on to the international scene at

the Beijing Olympics eight years earlier, stunning the
world when he recorded the fastest ever times in
the 100m, 200m and relay. Then, four years later, he
was the superstar of the London Games, sprinting to
another three gold medals.

Now in Rio, with the 100m and 200m golds
already safely packed away in his suitcase, Usain
had the chance to record historic treble. In the
relay, he wanted to give the fans one spectacular last
performance to remember.

He took a deep breath. He had been here so many
times before, in so many high-pressure races, but
he couldn't help but feel a little nervous. Unlike the
individual events where he could control his own
destiny, he relied on his teammates in the relay. Each
team was made up of four athletes, and Usain would
need his fellow Jamaicans to be on top form if they
were to win gold. Luckily, in Asafa Powell, Yohan
Blake and Nickel Ashmeade, he knew his country
had some of the fastest men on the planet.

It was nearly time. In less than forty seconds, his
Olympic career would be over.

'Come on, boys. Just get the baton safely round to me – then I'll do the rest,' said Usain, who would run the last leg of the relay.

No one could hear a word he said, though. It was too loud from all the fans' screaming.

At last the crowd fell silent as they waited for the starter's gun.

Bang!

The crowd roared. They were off.

Asafa burst out of the blocks. Usain was standing on the far side of the track, but he could see that his teammate was running a great first leg. Jamaica were neck and neck with the USA as Asafa handed the baton to Yohan Blake.

Immediately to Yohan's left was the American Justin Gatlin, Usain's great rival. They had enjoyed some terrific battles over the years, but Usain had always held the upper hand – and he was desperate to keep it that way tonight.

'Come on,' he said. 'Run like the wind.'

There was still nothing to choose between the two teams as Nickel took the baton for the third leg. Usain got into position. He couldn't watch any more. Instead, he was facing forward and waiting for the call.

'Go!' Nickel shouted. That was his signal.

Usain started running. He held his left arm out behind him as he started to build up speed. Nickel put the baton into his hand.

Usain looked to his left and right. He was directly in line with the USA and Japan, with Canada just behind them. It couldn't have been any closer.

He switched the baton to his right hand and – whoosh! – he was off. With his knees high in the air and arms pumping, he broke into full stride.

In the blink of an eye, he had opened up a one-metre gap. He knew no one could catch him now. Ever since his sports coach at primary school had told him to stop playing cricket and take up athletics, it had almost always been the same story – once he hit the front, he was unbeatable.

The race was all over long before Usain reached the finish line. Japan, the USA, Canada and the rest were blown away.

Usain was the Olympic champion again!

As he crossed the line one last time, he raised his right arm triumphantly in the air before giving a three-finger salute. One finger for each of his gold medals in Rio.

'Woooo-hoooo!'

But Usain didn't stop there. He kept on running, all the way to the Jamaican fans who were wildly waving their yellow, green and black flags in the stands. He was swallowed up in a sea of hugs.

Asafa, Yohan and Nickel quickly arrived on the scene. Cue more hugs.

'Yes, boys, we did it!'

'Jamaica, top of the world – again.'

Draped in a Jamaican flag, Usain set off with his teammates on a victory lap, but while they had run around the track in just 37.27 seconds in the relay, this lap took closer to thirty minutes this time around! Usain wanted to soak up every single second. He waved to the crowd, blew kisses and showed off some nimble footwork with his dance moves.

Finally, he gave the fans the moment they had all

been waiting for – the Lightning Bolt. It was his signature move that everyone knew. He pointed up with his left arm while keeping his right arm down, as if he was firing a bolt to the sky. The fans yelled their approval, many of them copying the pose.

There was time for one last interview.

'It's a brilliant feeling. It's been a long road. I'm happy, but I'm relieved.'

He signed off by announcing what everyone had been saying for years.

'There you go, I am the greatest.'

CATCH UP WITH THE BRILLIANT FOOTBALL HEROES SERIES

RONALDO

MESSI

The Rocket tells of how Cristiano Ronaldo overcame poverty and childhood illness to become one of the best football players ever. Escaping the hot streets of Madeira, Ronaldo first proved himself as a wonder-kid at Manchester United under Sir Alex Ferguson, before becoming a legend for Real Madrid and Portugal. This is the story of how the gifted boy became a man, a team-player and a legend.

978 1 78606 405 9
£5. 99

Lionel Messi is a legend – Barcelona's star player and the world's best footballer. But when he was young, he was so small that his friends would call him 'Little Leo' and coaches worried he wasn't big enough to play. Yet through bravery, talent and hard work, he proved them all wrong. *Little Lion* tells the magical story of how the tiniest boy in South America grew up to become the greatest player on earth.

978 1 78606 379 3
£5. 99

COLLECT THEM ALL

NEYMAR

POGBA

Neymar da Silva Santos Júnior is the boy with the big smile who carries the hopes of Brazil on his shoulders. Neymar now stands alongside Pelé and Ronaldinho as a Brazilian footballing hero. Bidding a fond farewell to his home in São Paolo, Neymar's dreams finally came true when he joined Barcelona. Now, alongside Messi and Suárez, he is part of the most feared attacking trident in the game. This is the heart-warming true story of Neymar's road to glory.

978 1 78606 379 3
£5. 99

Paul Pogba: Pogboom tells the exciting story of how French wonder-kid Paul Pogba became Europe's best young player, and finally fulfilled his dream of returning to his boyhood club Manchester United in a world-record transfer. The sky is the limit for United's new star.

978 1 78606 379 3
£5. 99

COLLECT THEM ALL

INIESTA

GIGGS

Andrés was always smaller than his friends, but he refused to let that stop him becoming one of the most special footballers of all time. *Andrés Iniesta: The Illusionist* tells of how his talent and hard work shone through as he rose through the ranks to become captain of the greatest Barcelona side ever, and score the winning goal in the World Cup final for Spain.

978 1 78606 380 9
£5.99

Ryan Giggs: Wing Wizard is the classic story of one of Manchester United's all-time heroes. As a teenager, he was so brilliant that Sir Alex Ferguson turned up at his front door to sign him – and the rest is history. A dazzlingly skilful winger, and one of the most decorated players ever, Ryan Giggs is a true Premier League legend.

978 1 78606 378 6
£5.99

COLLECT THEM ALL

AGÜERO

GERRARD

The Little Genius is the tale of the boy who would go on to change football history forever. His dramatic ninety-fourth minute goal on the final day of the 2012/13 season, to snatch the title from under rivals Manchester United's noses, was the most electric moment in Premier League history. This is how the small boy from Argentina became the biggest hero of all.

978 1 78606 218 5
£5.99

Steven Gerrard: Captain Fantastic tells of how a young boy from Merseyside overcame personal tragedy in the Hillsborough disaster to make his dream of playing for Liverpool FC come true. But that boy was no ordinary footballer; he would go on to captain his club for over a decade, inspiring their legendary Champions League FA Cup wins along the way. This is the story of Steven Gerrard, Liverpool's greatest ever player.

978 1 78606 219 2
£5.99

COLLECT THEM ALL

IBRAHIMOVIĆ

SÁNCHEZ

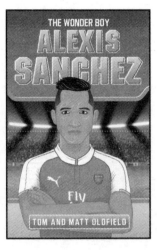

Zlatan Ibrahimović: Red Devil follows the Swedish superstar on his amazing journey from the tough streets of Malmö to becoming the deadly striker at Manchester United. Along the way he has been a star for Juventus, Inter Milan, Barcelona, and Paris Saint-Germain, as well as becoming Sweden's all-time leading goal scorer. This is the story of one of a generation's finest footballers.

978 1 78606 217 8
£5.99

Alexis Sánchez: The Wonder Boy tells the story of the Arsenal superstar's incredible journey from the streets of Tocopilla to become 'The Boy Wonder', a national hero, and one of the most talented players in the world. With his pace, skill and eye for a goal, Alexis is now one of the Premier League's biggest stars. The story is every bit as exciting as the player.

978 1 78606 013 6
£5.99

COLLECT THEM ALL

SUÁREZ

HAZARD

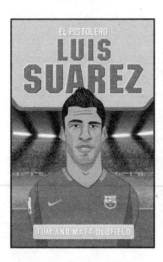

Luis Suárez: El Pistolero follows the Uruguayan's winding path from love-struck youngster to Liverpool hero to Barcelona star. Grabbing goals and headlines along the way, Luis chased his dreams and became a Champions League winner. This is the inspiring story of how the world's deadliest striker made his mark.

978 1 78606 012 9
£5.99

Eden Hazard: The Boy in Blue is the thrilling tale of how the wing wizard went from local wonder kid to league champion. With the support of his football-obsessed family, Eden worked hard to develop his amazing dribbling skills and earn his dream transfer to Chelsea.

978 1 78606 014 3
£5.99

COLLECT THEM ALL

BALE

ROONEY

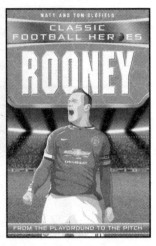

Gareth Bale: The Boy Who Became a Galáctico tracks the Welsh wizard's impressive rise from talented schoolboy to Real Madrid star. This is the inspiring story of how Bale beat the odds and became the most expensive player in football history.

978 1 78418 645 7
£5.99

Wayne Rooney: Captain of England tells the action-packed story of one boy's journey from the streets of Croxteth to one of the biggest stages in world football. This heartwarming book tracks Rooney's fairytale rise from child superstar to Everton hero to Manchester United legend.

978 1 78418 647 0
£5.99

COLLECT THEM ALL

STERLING

Raheem Sterling: Young Lion
is the exciting tale of a boy
who followed his passion and
became one of the most dynamic
young players in world football,
winning the hearts of Liverpool
and England fans along the
way. Relive Sterling's whirlwind
journey in this uplifting story.

978 1 78418 646 3
£5.99